# Construction play

CHRIS HEALD

**Published by Scholastic Ltd,**
Villiers House,
Clarendon Avenue,
Leamington Spa,
Warwickshire CV32 5PR

3 4 5 6 7 8 9 9 0 1 2 3 4 5 6

**Author**
Chris Heald

**Editor**
Sally Gray

**Series designer**
Lynne Joesbury

**Designer**
Claire Belcher

**Illustrations**
Rachel Connor

**Cover photograph**
Fiona Pragoff

Designed using Adobe Pagemaker

British Library Cataloguing-in-Publication Data
A catalogue record for this book is available from the British Library.

ISBN 0-590-53687-7

# CONTENTS

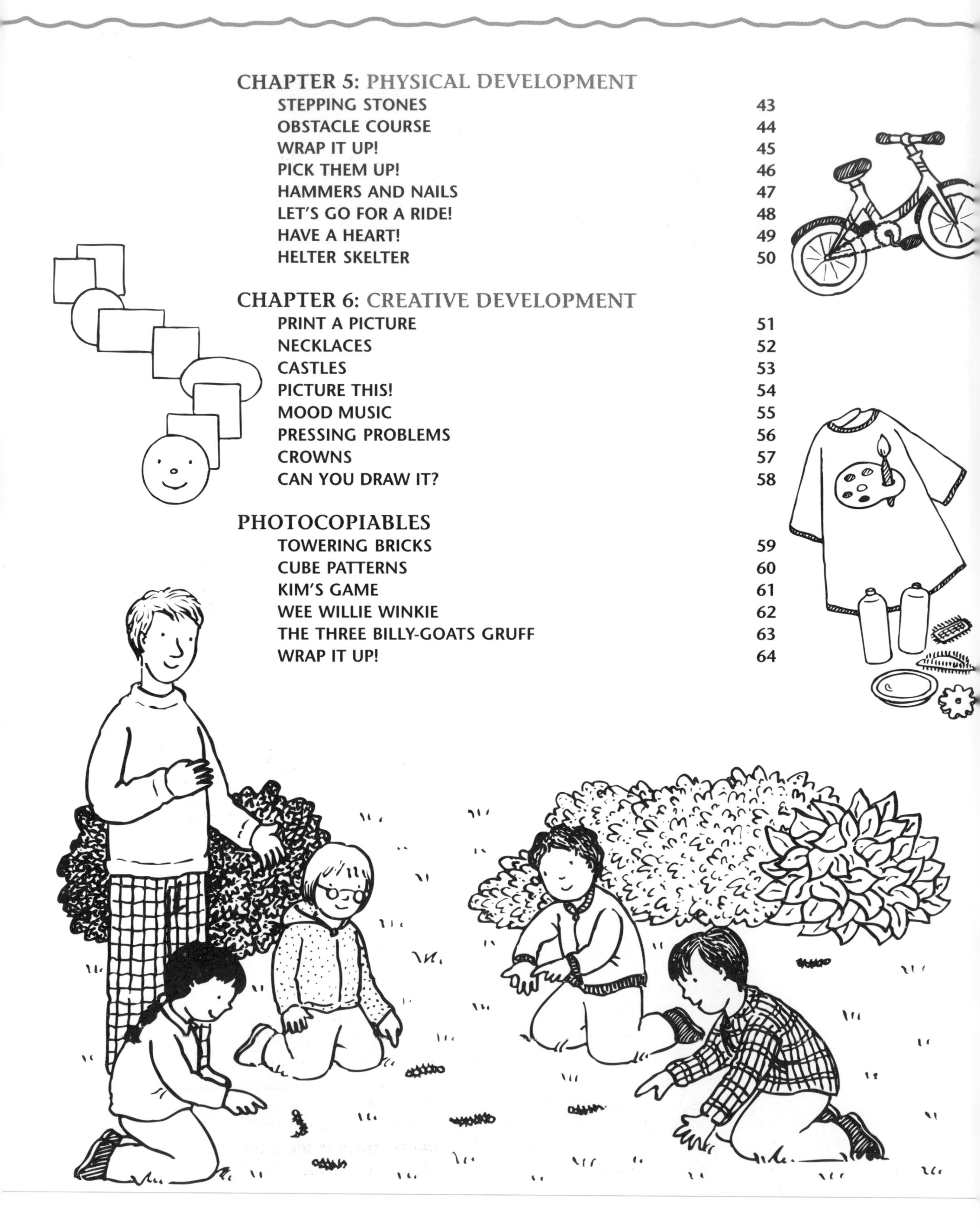

## CHAPTER 5: PHYSICAL DEVELOPMENT



## CHAPTER 6: CREATIVE DEVELOPMENT



## PHOTOCOPIABLES

# INTRODUCTION

A variety of bricks and construction toys are usually offered in playgroups/nurseries and reception classes. Construction materials are flexible and can be used to create whatever the children need for their play. They are an essential ingredient of free-play, encouraging developing thought processes as well as fine motor skills.

## Learning through play

The Qualifications and Curriculum Authority (QCA) have outlined a set of 'Early Learning Gorlas' which are goals for children's learning by the time they enter compulsory education.

The Early Learning Goals cover traditional expectations of what an average child should be able to do, and the skills they should develop. This will vary from child to child across the age range, depending on the children's individual abilities and the experiences that they have had.

The Early Learning Goals are presented as six Areas of Learning; each of which has been allocated a chapter in this book.

Free-play is vital in early years learning and should form a large part of any good nursery provision. This does not mean leaving children alone to play while the adults do something else, but means offering children a variety of experiences which enable them to find out for themselves the way things work. Adults need to play alongside children, finding out what they understand, suggesting ways of extending their understanding and helping them to progress. Good early years provision of any kind will encourage children to be adventurous but safe, providing an environment which will stimulate and develop the skills and knowledge of the young child.

## Setting up the environment

The environment for construction play needs to be comfortable and spacious. Children need to be able to spread out and build sizeable objects, with cars, trains and people all brought into the play. Carpet on an open floor space is ideal with some large cushions or bean-bags.

It is vitally important to have plenty of bricks and components so that the children are not frustrated in their attempts to bring their ideas to fruition. If you have cards and pictures for children to copy ensure that all the pieces necessary are available for their use.

## Storage

Construction toys are best kept in their own storage box or container, properly labelled so that they are readily available for use. It can be frustrating for children to have to search through a large toybox for the few essential components which have fallen to the bottom and they may give up in disgust! Store the equipment so that the children are able to select their own construction toy and put it away afterwards. A trolley which holds up to twelve deep plastic trays is ideal for construction toys and these are available from most educational suppliers.

## Observation and assessment

In order to observe and assess, it is first necessary to understand what you can expect of the children. QCA's Early Learning Goals for learning point us towards reasonable expectations for pre-school children. These expectations may then be used as a guide to plan the assessment of your group of children.

Keep detailed records of the individuals in your care. Make regular observations of them at play and as they perform set tasks and use this information to help you decide what further experiences they need. This information should be kept to form part of the child's Record of Achievement for their early years.

## Using adult helpers

Adult interaction is essential to young children. It is a strong motivating force both for learning and behaviour. A sensitive adult will work alongside the children, allowing them to take the lead and acting as an enabler, offering suggestions and new experiences. The most important tool for an adult helper is their questioning technique. Open questions should be asked – those which do not have a simple 'yes' or 'no' answer, but which invite the child to tell you at length about their experience. For instance, 'Did you like that?' is a question which may lead to a 'yes' or 'no' answer, whereas, 'What are you doing?' needs an explanation from the child and can result in a conversation.

## Types of construction sets

Construction equipment may be classified into a number of different types. Where possible, nurseries and playgroups should aim to have a variety of different types so that the children can have the maximum choice in their play. Costs vary, but all the ones mentioned below are hard-wearing and stand up well to extended use by young children.

The following list classifies construction equipment into different categories:

**Large construction equipment for building child-sized vehicles, houses etc:**
Quadro, NES Arnold Hollow Bricks, NES Arnold Plasbrics, Big Waffle Blocks, Galt Extra large playbricks, Snap Land, Galt Lincabricks, Babybric, Ludocyl.

**Flexible, making outline framework:**
Construct-O-Straws, Cleversticks, Tactic, Fun Straws, Popoids, Zoketts, Mini-Edra, Sonos, Systema.

**Shaped bricks which snap together, some soft, some firm:**
Waffle Blocks, Poly-M, Duplo, LEGO, LEGO Dacta, Reo-Click, Mega Bloks, Mobilo, Ascobric, Big Blocks, Scobar, Batisco, Lasy, Puzzle Pies.

**Classic wooden, plain or painted, bricks – held together only by gravity and correct placement:**
Galt playbricks, Galt building blocks, Galt wooden cubes, Plastic building bricks (available from NES Arnold).

**Sets which include figures of people/animals:**
Popoids, Poly-M, Mega Bloks, Wee Waffle blocks, Sticklebricks, LEGO, Duplo, Dacta, Mobilo, Manetico, Magnetic construction system (available from Galt).

**Flat Geometric shapes which fit together to make solid shapes:**
Polydron, Clixi, Lokko, Googolplex.

**Construction environments:**
Duplo house, zoo, hospital, farm and so on, LittleTikes house, castle, farm, Luna Park.

**Road, waterway and rail construction:**
LEGO and Duplo railways, Little Tikes roadway/railway, Brio railway sets, Waterway Play System, Aquaplay Water System.

**Construction with nuts and bolts and with tools:**
LEGO Toolo, Brio-Mec, Baufix, Hanse Tec, Creato, Junior Meccano, Asmeca, Axis.

**Slide into slot construction:**
Glisso, Klondikers, Interstar, Galt Playplax, Flexiblocks, Polydron Octoplay, Criss-Cross, Star-Stack, Starburst, Geo-Links.

**Magnetic construction:**
Manetico, Magnetic blocks.

**Gears:**
Luna Park, Georello, Rotello.

The following is a list of some of the suppliers that stock a range of construction equipment:

**Asco Educational Supplies Ltd**
19 Lockwood Way, Parkside Lane
Leeds LS11 5TH

**Edco**
1 Mallusk Park, Mallusk Road
Newtownabbey, Co Antrim
BT36 4GW

**Hope Education**
Orb Mill, Huddersfield Road
Waterhead, Oldham,
Lancs OL4 2ST
**Galt Educational**
Orb Mill, Culvert Street
Waterhead, Oldham,
Lancs OL4 2ST
**NES Arnold Ltd**
Ludlow Hill Road
West Bridgford
Nottingham
NG2 6HD
**Step by Step**
Lavenham Road
Beeches Trading Estate
Yate, Bristol BS17 5QS
**Yorkshire Purchasing Organisation**
41 Industrial Park
Wakefield WF2 0XE

## Links with home

Communication between your group and the children's home environment is very important – the more links which can be created the better your children will settle. It is important to be approachable, for some parents it is the first time they have left their child in someone else's care and they are naturally apprehensive. Home visits are an excellent idea if they can be arranged and staff can be freed to do it. If possible, when the children are new to your group, invite parents to stay for a while to help the child settle in. Why not invite parents to come and work with the children? The benefits of this are twofold – an extra pair of hands is always useful to have and the parents also see how things are done in your setting, bridging the gap between

nursery/playgroup and the home. Good communication may also take the written form – have some leaflets printed which tell new parents all about the service you offer, and give one to any parent who makes an enquiry. Send a regular newsletter home with the children telling parents what you have been doing. Put a different notice up every week, telling parents one of the things you will be doing this week. Encourage the children to bring items from home and talk to the other children about them.

## Health and safety

Throughout the book, you will notice a (CARE!) warning which highlights activities that require careful supervision.

Construction toys will need to be washed and sterilised at regular intervals to make sure that they are not passing germs from child to child. Other considerations include the size of pieces in your construction. Could a young child swallow one? Stick one in her ear or up her nose? Always consult the product guidelines about ages of suitability for playing with any toy, and stick to them.

Consideration also needs to be given to the safety of adults and other children who walk around your base. Do not let children build with construction in a narrow corridor or just behind a door which leads to another room.

Tools such as hammers, screwdrivers, nails and screws should always be stored out of the reach of young children, and they should only use them with one-to-one adult supervision.

## How to use this book

This book is divided into six chapters, organised into the six Areas of Learning identified for the under-fives by the School Curriculum and Assessment Authority. There are eight activities under each chapter heading, aimed to develop skills and knowledge in the designated area. Although the activities will have a main focus in one of the areas, the potential for learning across the curriculum will often be realised simultaneously and other skills may be the focus of the suggested follow-up activities. This integrated approach is a very good way for young children to learn.

The Topic Web on page 10 shows all the activities, with their page reference, listed under their relevant Area of Learning.

Use this book as you would use a recipe book, adding your own personal touches and ideas to the outline of the activity. Do not expect very young children to be interested in the end product of any activity. Young children want to experiment with tools and materials and techniques. They are learning whilst they actively cut, stick, paint, poke with sticks, dab with sponges and so on. Listen to your children and let them take you where they want to go, to explore areas which interest them, since this is the way to produce children who are highly motivated to learn.

## CONSTRUCTION PLAY

### PERSONAL AND SOCIAL DEVELOPMENT

### LANGUAGE AND LITERACY



### PHYSICAL DEVELOPMENT

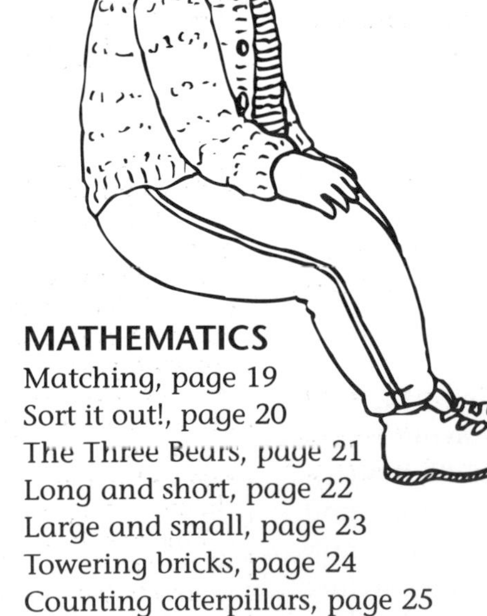

### KNOWLEDGE AND UNDERSTANDING OF THE WORLD



### MATHEMATICS



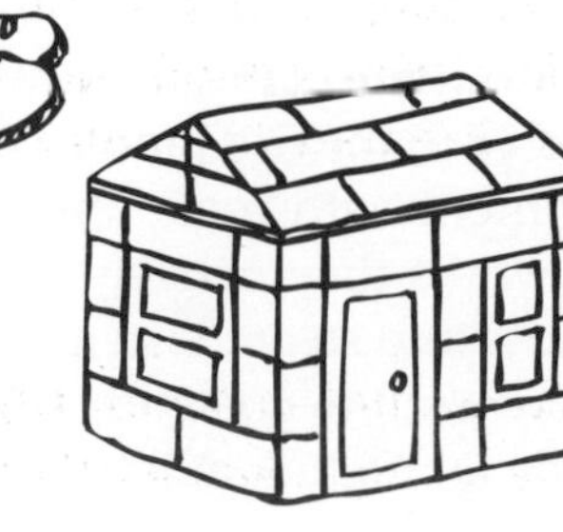

### CREATIVE DEVELOPMENT

***The activities in this chapter provide contexts to develop all the essential literacy skills for young children. In 'Listen carefully!' the children will use bricks and play figures to develop listening skills, and the skills of writing and speaking are addressed in 'Making people' and 'What are you doing?'.***

# HUMPTY DUMPTY

***Learning objective***
*To listen and respond appropriately to a well-known nursery rhyme.*

***Group size***
*Up to six children working together.*

## What you need

A toy which can act as Humpty Dumpty. This could even be a cushion with eyes and nose sewn onto it with wool. A construction set which includes large, simple bricks which resemble house-bricks and can be used to build a wall, such as Quadro or Galt Extra large playbricks.

## Setting up

Make sure the toy you are using will 'sit' on top of a row of the bricks you are using.

## What to do

Show the children the toy Humpty Dumpty and say the rhyme 'Humpty Dumpty' together.

Invite the children to make a wall for Humpty Dumpty to sit on and fall off. Join in the play and help the children to understand how to make a wall which will not fall down by alternating the joins in the bricks.

When the wall has been built, say the rhyme again and encourage the children to take turns putting Humpty on the wall and knocking him off on cue.

## Questions to ask

How did you make your wall stay together? Which bricks did you use? What happened to Humpty Dumpty? How do you think he felt when he was knocked off the wall? What happens to you when you fall over? How do you feel? What could you do to help Humpty Dumpty?

## For younger children

Younger children may need more adult help when building their wall though they will enjoy knocking Humpty off the wall with equal vigour! Make sure you provide large easily manipulated bricks for them to use.

## For older children

Ask older children to look at a book that shows the rhyme. Help them to pick out some of the familiar words, using initial sounds to make guesses at the difficult words.

**Follow-up activities**

- Let the children try to write the words or draw a series of pictures that tell the story of the nursery rhyme.
- Use bricks and paint to print a large picture of a wall. Make a Humpty Dumpty figure from collage materials to sit on top of the wall. Complete the display by putting some nursery rhyme books underneath.

# LISTEN CAREFULLY!

***Learning objective***
*To listen attentively and follow instructions.*

***Group size***
*Six children.*

## What you need
Any construction set with figures. A quiet area.

## Setting up
Allocate a figure for each child and one for yourself. Discuss with the children what the word 'figure' means if you intend to use this word.

## What to do
Put the construction set in the middle of the table. Explain to the children that you want them to listen very carefully to what you are going to say because you are going to tell them what you want them to do with their figures. Give the children some directions such as: 'I want you to put your figure on top of a red brick'. Wait for them to do this, and then show them with your figure: 'Yes, here's my figure standing on top of a red brick'.

Use a variety of 'positional' words such as: lying, sitting and standing with, beside, in, and so on. Also, vary the colours and shapes of bricks that you choose. Only give the children a visual clue after they have had time to listen and decide what they are going to do.

## Questions to ask
Where is the red brick? Where have you put your figure? What sort of figure have you got? Can you remember where we last put our figures? Where do you think they could go next? Can you tell your friend where to put their figure?

## For younger children
Younger children may find it easier to deal with just one concept, such as colour. For instance, ask if they could put the figure on top of a red brick, and repeat this with all the colours available in the set.

## For older children
Bring in an element of choice with older children, such as put your figure on top of a red or a blue brick. Encourage them to build up a sequence of actions.

**Follow-up activities**
- During story time ask the children to place themselves around the room in a similar way to how they had placed their figures earlier. For example, 'Sachin go and sit on the blue stool'.
- Record some instructions on tape for the children to listen to. Include some silly ones such as 'waggle your bottom'. This can then progress to more complex instructions such as: 'lie on your tummy and crawl'.
- Play a listening game – three children stand with their backs to the group, one of them says 'Hello' and the others have to guess who it was.

# MAKING PEOPLE

***Learning objective***
*To begin to use familiar words and letters to communicate meaning.*

***Group size***
*Six children.*

## What you need
A construction set which has heads, torsos, arms and legs which can be used to make humanoid shapes. Examples are Popoids, Sticklebricks or Mobilo. A large or full-length unbreakable mirror. Sheets of paper, brightly coloured felt-tipped pens.

## Setting up
Cut the paper into pieces about 12cm by 10cm. Fold one piece in half lengthways. Make sure that there are enough pieces to provide a choice for your group.

## What to do
Look in the mirror with the children and talk about what they can see. Talk about how many arms and legs and heads people have.

Ask the children to try and make a person using the pieces they have available, making sure that they have all their main body parts. Join in and make one yourself. Give the children plenty of time to try different combinations of heads and limbs, then ask them to choose the best one they have made.

Ask each child to choose a name for their person. It could be a made-up one or a real person's name. Then show the children how to fold a piece of paper like yours and write the name on the label. Encourage them to 'have a go' at the writing, helping them to make the letter sounds and form their letters correctly.

## Questions to ask
What would happen if your person only had one leg/no head? How many arms/legs has your person got? What do you like best about your person? What name have you given your person? What rhymes with your person's name?

## For younger children
Younger children may find it easier to name their figures after themselves, so that when they write the name the word is familiar.

## For older children
Invite older children to make a robot family together with robot pets.

**Follow-up activities**
- Ask the children if they can design a house or a garden for their person using reclaimed materials.
- Make aliens and monsters in different coloured Plasticine with lots of heads and limbs.
- Print by dipping geometrically-shaped bricks in paint and ask the children if they can make these into a person.

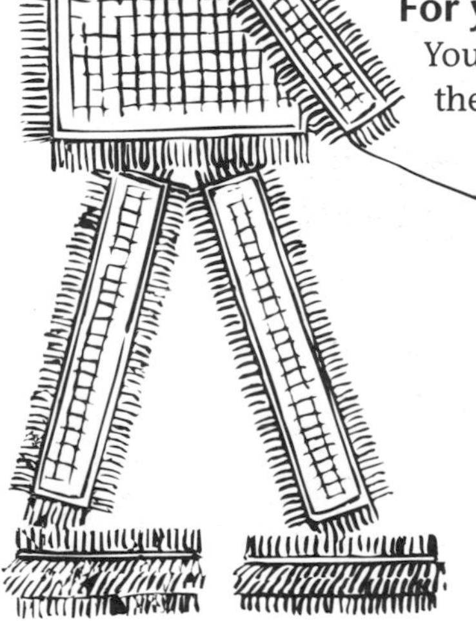

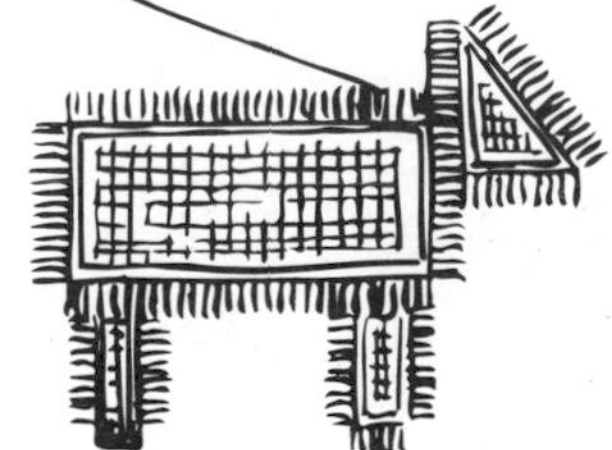

# WHAT ARE YOU DOING?

*Learning objective*
*To develop speaking skills in response to questions.*

*Group size*
*Four children.*

## What you need

A construction toy which is new to your group. Somewhere to sit and talk quietly, with a table to work on.

## Setting up

Do not bring out the new toy until you have your group settled.

## What to do

Show the children the new construction toy and ask them to play with it. Observe the children while they are finding out about how it works and ask them some questions which need an explanation and cannot be answered with 'yes' or 'no' or a gesture. If the children give you a one-word answer, take their word, add some description to it and use it to ask a question which needs another answer for example: 'Yes, I can see it's a car, a car I could ride to the seaside in. Where would you like to go in it?'.

When a child finds answering difficult, try to suggest a choice of answers to help them find the words they need.

## Questions to ask

Can you tell me what you are making? Who is it for? What could you make with these bricks? How did you make that model? When you've finished that model, what do you want to make next?

## For younger children

Younger children may need some more help with answering the questions. Help them by offering them some choices to develop their vocabulary. They may be so fascinated by the new toy that they only start to talk about it towards the end of the session.

## For older children

Older and more able children could work towards creative writing, making a model and then letting their pencil talk about what they have made. Sometimes these pencil marks are unintelligible to formal writers, but as long as the child can 'read' it to you, accept this as emergent writing.

**Follow-up activities**

- Ask the children to describe their models to the children in another group. Can they identify whose model is whose? How?
- Place a cassette-recorder with the construction play. Encourage the children to record what they want to say about their models.

# FUN WITH WHEELS

***Learning objective***
*To develop the ability to use books to find out information.*

***Group size***
*Four children.*

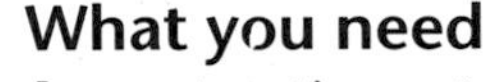

## What you need

A construction set with wheels, such as Mobilo, Brio-Mec or Poly-M. Pictures of a variety of vehicles cut from magazines and stuck on to sturdy card. Books about vehicles. A carpeted area.

## Setting up

Check that there are enough pieces to provide a choice for each child. Ask the children to get out the construction set and put it somewhere that they can all work comfortably.

## What to do

Suggest that the children tip all the pieces out on to the carpet to allow them to be seen clearly. Show the children the pictures and ask them if they know what each one is called.

Invite them to try to make a car like the one in the picture. When the cars have been made to each child's satisfaction, push them across the carpet to see if the wheels work. Have another look at the books to find some more pictures of things with wheels.

## Questions to ask

What sort of car/lorry did you make? How did you make your car/ lorry? Where is it going? Can you make it move? How? What makes a real car move? How many wheels are on your lorry? Who could ride in it? What do you like about the car you have made?

## For younger children

Allow younger children to play freely with the construction set first before encouraging them to make a car. Join in the play with the children, helping them with their ideas.

## For older children

Provide a more intricate construction set for these children to use. Encourage them to make an environment for their vehicles – such as a petrol station or a street.

**Follow-up activities**

- Provide a large sheet of paper, with trays of different colours of paint. Ask the children to dip the wheels of their vehicle in paint, pushing it across the paper to make tracks.
- Sort the vehicles into sets according to the number of wheels, by colour and so on.
- Ask the children to draw their model. Make a book of the drawings and leave it in the book area for everyone to read.

# BUILDING SIGHTS

***Learning objective***
*To use construction play to develop verbal sequencing skills.*

***Group size***
*Six children.*

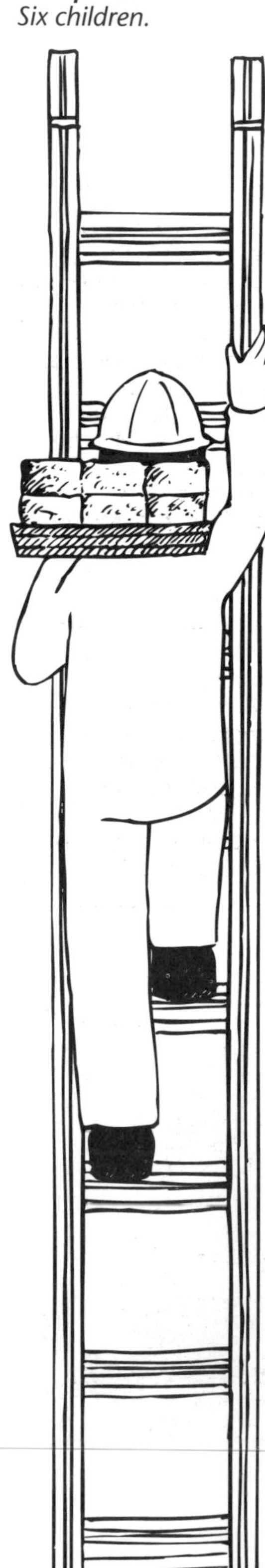

## What you need

A local building site where there are houses in various stages of construction. Ideally, a set of pictures showing the various stages of building a house. A construction set which can be used for building a house, such as LEGO or Duplo. Other construction sets which could be used for scaffolding and so on (such as Construct-O-straws).

## Setting up

Arrange to go for a walk to observe a nearby building site to look at the houses being built (from a safe distance). Try to go there yourself beforehand and take photographs of houses in various stages of completion, from the laying of the foundations to the finished product. Get prints made ready for the day of the children's visit. Make sure you have enough bricks for the children to build their own versions of what they have seen.

## What to do

Go for a walk to a local building site to observe some houses being built. Make sure there are plenty of adults accompanying the children and observe from a safe distance.

When you return to your base, talk about what you have seen. Show the children the photographs you have taken, and talk about the different stages there are in the building of a house. Invite the children to have a go at building a house. As they work, talk about the different stages that need to be gone through.

## Questions to ask

What sort of jobs did you see being done? What tools did you see? What machines did you see? What did the site look like? How was a new house started? What happened next? What do you think are the last things to be done to a house?

## For younger children

Younger children will enjoy a visit to a building site and will benefit from talking about it. Follow the visit with some free play with lots of different construction toys and some figures.

## For older children

Provide some miniature real bricks and water soluble mortar. (These 'Brick Building Systems' and 'Mortar sets' are available from Hope Education, see page 8 for the address.) Older children would also enjoy designing and making houses with gardens. Gardens are easily made using seed trays, peat-free compost, plants and reclaimed materials.

**Follow-up activities**

- Using a cardboard box as a small room, let the children decorate it with wallpaper and paints. They could then use doll's house furniture or attempt to make furniture from reclaimed materials.
- Cut 'bricks' out of brightly coloured paper and ask the children to make and stick brick patterns onto black paper.
- Read the story *Who's afraid of the big bad wolf* by Tony Bradman (Little Mammoth) and talk about the reasons why some of the houses fell down while the brick house stayed together.

# PATH MAKER

***Learning objective***
*To enjoy a story, relating it to personal experience.*

***Group size***
*Six children.*

## What you need
The book *Going on a Bear Hunt* by Michael Rosen (Walker Books). A large construction set made of wood or plastic which includes planks and supports, such as the Edra system. An area where the children can construct a sizeable pathway to walk along.

## Setting up
Make sure the children can work independently by storing the bricks in wheeled containers which they can handle easily.

## What to do
Read the story together with your group at least twice. Ask the children if they think they can build a pathway to take them through dry grass, squelchy mud and so on. Encourage them to lay out the planks in their own design and walk along them, talking about which imaginary area they are going through. Finally sit down and read the book again, encouraging the children to join in with the words they recognise.

## Questions to ask
Where are you now? What might live in that sticky mud? What might happen if you step off the safe path? What do you think we will find at the end of the pathway? Which was your favourite part of the book?

## For younger children
Younger children will enjoy the repetition in the story and some may be able to join in. Show them how to lay out the materials to make a kind of path. Make the relevant 'squelchy' or 'squishy' noises with them as they walk over the planks.

## For older children
Having used the construction set and listened to the story, older children could be asked to draw a simple map showing the path they took through all the different obstacles.

**Follow-up activities**
- Encourage the children to paint large pieces of wallpaper to resemble the obstacles encountered on the bear-hunt. Place these on the floor in the role-play area with your construction set.
- Ask the children to choose suitable percussion instruments to create the sound-effects of the story while you read it aloud.
- Put a smaller construction set in some damp sand and suggest that the children make pathways from one side to the other.

# WHAT WOULD HAPPEN IF...?

*Learning objective*
*To use construction toys to predict what will happen next.*

*Group size*
*Up to eight children.*

## What you need
A construction set made from soft foam such as Maxisoft Blocks. The song 'I went to school one morning' in *This Little Puffin* compiled by Elizabeth Matterson (Puffin).

## Setting up
Ensure that your group wear plimsolls or are barefoot for this activity. Place your box of soft bricks close by. Ensure your group is familiar with the actions of the song.

## What to do
Sing the song and perform the actions in the normal way, then ask your group to sit down in a circle. Ask them what they think would happen if they were to sing the song with a brick balanced on their heads, or under their chins, or held between their feet/knees/elbows. Then ask each child to choose a brick and try. Can they make a shape with several bricks which will be easy to balance?

## Questions to ask
What did you find easiest to do? What was hardest to do? Why? What happened when you put the brick on your head? What happened when you had to jump? How could you stop the brick from falling? What was the funniest thing you tried to do?

## For younger children
It will be more appropriate for younger children to do this activity without the added complication of remembering the song. Sit the children in a circle and ask if they can hold a brick in one hand and hop, (let them all try), hold one between their feet and jump, or balance one on their head and walk. Make sure you praise each child's attempts.

## For older children
Older children can be asked from the start to try to make a shape with the bricks which will allow them to jump, hop or skip, keeping the bricks in place. They could then test a range of PE equipment such as bean-bags, balls and quoits to see which one they think is best.

**Follow-up activities**
- Do some colour-mixing and ask the children to predict what colour they are going to make before they actually mix the colours together.
- Look at raw eggs (CARE! some children are allergic to eggs) and ask the children to predict what will happen to the colour and texture when they are cooked.
- Plant three pots of seeds in peat-free compost and treat them in three different ways for example: too much water/enough water/not enough water. Ask the children to predict which pot will grow the best.

# MATHEMATICS

***Construction toys are an exciting resource for children to use whilst developing their mathematical skills. Making snakes to develop comparative language in 'Long and short' and improving counting and shape recognition skills in 'Counting caterpillars' are just some of the suggestions that follow.***

# MATCHING

***Learning objective***
*To recognise and recreate shape patterns.*

***Group size***
*Four children.*

## What you need

Ten bricks for each child in your group. A comfortable carpeted area.

## Setting up

Ensure that each child has ten identical bricks. To do this, ask them to find ten bricks which are the same as yours.

## What to do

Start by asking the children to see what they can make with their ten bricks. Encourage each child to make something different. Show them some examples by joining in and making several different things with your bricks such as an aeroplane, a boat, a bridge and so on.

Ask the children to work in pairs and see if they can make a model the same as their partner's – a 'twin' model. To help them understand what you mean, work alongside them, copying one of their models. When they are all satisfied with their models talk about them together.

## Questions to ask

What have you made? How many bricks have you used? Is yours the same as hers? Where does this brick go if you want the model to be the same? Why do you like your model? What else could you make with these bricks? What shape is this brick?

## For younger children

Use fewer bricks with younger children and ask them to try to make two or three different things using the same number of bricks. They will probably find it extremely difficult to copy another child's model.

## For older children

Ask older children to work in pairs with a full construction set and instruction leaflets (laminated) to copy to make large models. Use the idea of making 'twin' models, as they find this interesting and it motivates them to produce models identical in colour and shape to the ones in the leaflets.

**Follow-up activities**
- Ask one of the children to explain to the group how she made her model, and why she chose to make what she did.
- Ask the children to draw their models. Display the drawings next to the finished models.
- Take a photograph of each child's model. Put them into a book as a reference of ideas which can be used with the leaflets from the construction set for other children to copy.

# SORT IT OUT!

***Learning objective***
*To learn how to sort objects using the criteria of shape and colour.*

***Group size***
*Eight children.*

## What you need
A construction toy with several different coloured or shaped pieces such as Luna Park. Containers to hold the different pieces. If you do not have enough of these, try making a partitioned box with stiff cardboard. A carpeted area.

## Setting up
Check that you have enough containers or segments to take all the different pieces. Keep some extra containers handy, as the children always seem to find more differences than adults. Allow plenty of time to develop the activity.

## What to do
Carefully empty all the pieces of the construction toy over your carpeted area. Ask them to decide which pieces should go together in which container, (perhaps based on shape or colour), then ask each child to try and think of another, different reason for sorting.

## Questions to ask
Why do you think that piece goes in there? What do you think that piece is useful for? What would you make with this piece? Where are you going to put it? Where would you put a green/blue/red one? What shapes could we put together?

## For younger children
Younger children can do this activity as part of tidying-up in their usual play. Only use large pieces and limit it to simple criteria such as colour.

## For older children
Older children can sort smaller, more intricate pieces. Encourage them to use more than one reason for sorting (for example, 'things that are red and square'). Ask them to draw sets of their own.

**Follow-up activities**
- Do some further sorting activities with buttons, sequins or any odds and ends you may be able to assemble (CARE! Ensure that young children do not put small objects in their nose, mouth or ears). It is important to talk about the reasons you could have for putting things together.
- Photocopy some bricks and ask the children to match the three-dimensional brick to the picture.

# THE THREE BEARS

***Learning objective***
*To use construction toy pieces to sequence for size.*

***Group size***
*Six children.*

## What you need

A construction toy which has large, medium sized and small parts. One large, one medium-sized and one small teddy bear. A version of *Goldilocks and the Three Bears*. A carpeted area. A plastic tray.

## Setting up

Take out six large, six medium and six small bricks from your set. Mix them up on the tray.

## What to do

Read the story to your group. Talk about the three teddy bears, pointing out that Baby Bear is small, Mummy Bear is larger and Daddy Bear is the largest. Ask the children if they can take turns to find the small bricks for Baby Bear, medium-sized bricks for Mummy Bear and large bricks for Daddy Bear. Let them choose a brick in turn and put it in front of the bear it belongs to. When they have each had a turn or two ask each child to make their own sequence of bricks from small to large.

## Questions to ask

Where are you going to put that brick? Why? What sort of brick goes in front of Daddy Bear? Which bear is your favourite? Tell me the story of 'The Three Bears'. How many people live in your house? Who is the smallest person in your house? Who wears the biggest shoes?

## For younger children

Younger children will enjoy hearing the story. Encourage them to order the actual bears from largest to smallest. Provide the children with plenty of opportunities in their play and when tidying-up to develop comparative language.

## For older children

Provide further opportunities for older children to sequence different objects for a variety of reasons. For example, they could sequence shades of colour from dark to light, or foods from favourite to least-favourite. Ask them to think of some ideas of their own.

**Follow-up activities**

- Provide small, medium and large dolls with clothes to match in the role-play area.
- Make a collection of natural objects such as leaves or pinecones and encourage the children to sequence them.
- Put three different sizes of paper in the painting area, and ask the children to choose the size they want.

# LONG AND SHORT

***Learning objective***
*To make and compare snakes of different lengths.*

***Group size***
*Four children.*

## What you need
A construction set which will fit end-to-end, such as Duplo, Mobilo, Zoketts or Sticklebricks (it is not necessary that they fix together, although that would be more convenient). Enough carpet space for a very long line of bricks!

## Setting up
Ensure the carpet area is free of obstructions. Keep back a few construction pieces out of sight.

## What to do
Begin by taking the children on a walk around your base. Encourage them to look for things that are long and short, emphasising the relevant vocabulary.

Group the children on the carpet and invite them to make a long snake with you. You will probably find that they use up all the pieces available to make a very long snake indeed. Now mention a short snake. How would they make that? The more enterprising may take a few pieces from the long snake, but if not, you could 'find' the pieces you have hidden, and give them to the children. Keep emphasising that one snake should be long and the other one short, or else you will end up with two long snakes and no short one.

## Questions to ask
Which snake took the longest time to make? Which snake took the shortest time to make? Why? How many pieces are in the short snake? And in the long snake? How can we measure how long each snake is? What could we use?

## For younger children
Work closely with younger children using the construction set to make different things. Point out to them when they have made something long or short and encourage them to use the words appropriately.

## For older children
Show older children how to use non-standard means of measuring to help them grasp length. They could measure how long their snake is by using books, or shoes.

**Follow-up activities**
- Put very long and very short laces with your threading beads.
- Read *Whistle for Willie* by Ezra Jack Keats (Picture Puffin).
Provide coloured chalks and let the children draw long and short lines on the outside play area.
- Make long and short snakes with Plasticine.

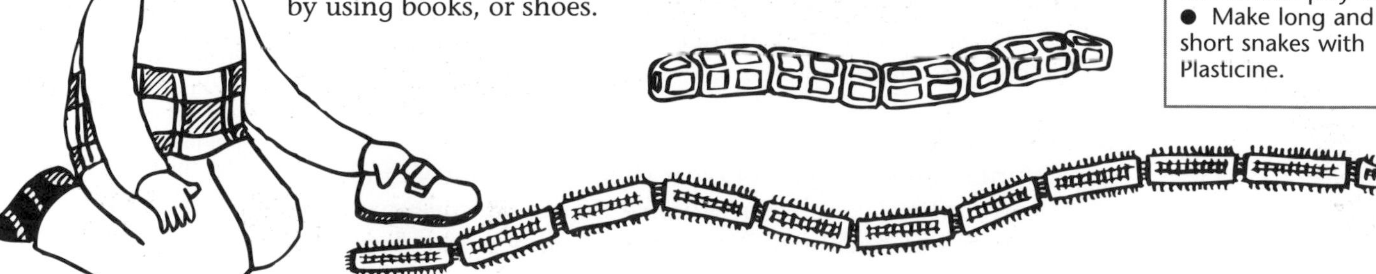

# LARGE AND SMALL

*Learning objective*
*To build and distinguish between a large and a small house.*

*Group size*
*Six children.*

## What you need
Two construction sets in containers, one with large pieces, such as Babybric or Large Wee Waffle bricks, and one with small pieces such as LEGO. Two pieces of paper/card for labels approximately 20cm by 7cm. A black felt-tipped pen. A small play figure such as from Playmobil/LEGO.

## Setting up
Write 'large' on one of your labels and 'small' on the other.

## What to do
Put the containers of bricks onto the carpet for the children to look at. Before they start to build, ask the children which set they would use to build a house large enough for themselves to play in, and which they would use to build a house small enough for the plastic figure. Stand the figure next to one of the children, so that the size difference is obvious. Show the children a piece from each set to help them decide which would be best, then let them build.

## Questions to ask
How many bricks did you use? How did you build the large house? What can you do in it? What would happen if you tried to get into the small house? What sort of house would a giant have? What size of house would be best for a mouse? What about a giraffe?

## For younger children
Invite younger children to build a house of any kind, using their choice of bricks. Use the opportunity to discuss differences in size as they occur.

## For older children
Extend the activity with older children by asking them to make furniture of different sizes to go in the two houses. They may also like to make sets of all kinds of large and small objects, such as socks, shoes, dolls and cars.

**Follow-up activities**
- Print on large and small pieces of paper with large and small brushes.
- Using old magazines, cut or tear out pictures of large objects and small objects and stick them on two separate pieces of paper labelled 'large' and 'small'.

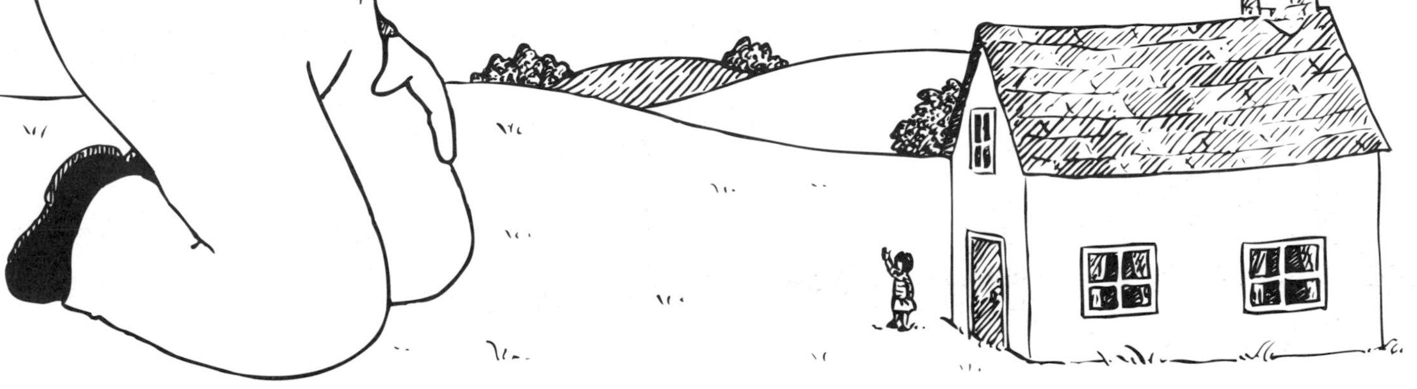

# TOWERING BRICKS

***Learning objective***
*To make tall and short towers of bricks.*

***Group size***
*Up to six children.*

## What you need
A large set of simple rectangular bricks. A carpeted area where the bricks can topple without too much noise.

## Setting up
Make sure there are enough bricks for each pair of children to make a tower at least as tall as themselves, and preferably taller.

## What to do
To begin with, allow the children some time for free play with the bricks. Encourage them to build towers and knock them over.

Ask the children if they can make a very short tower. When they have done this ask them if anyone can make a taller tower, perhaps as tall as one of the children. Invite the children to work together to make the tallest tower they possibly can. This will probably take most or all of the available bricks, so the children will need to co-operate with each other.

## Questions to ask
Which tower was the tallest? Which one was the shortest? Why? Can you make a tower the same size as one of the children in the group? Can you make a tower the same size as one of the adult helpers? Can you make it shorter/taller than him/her? How?

## For younger children
Allow younger children plenty of time to play freely with their bricks to develop their dexterity. Discuss the different sizes of the towers they build.

## For older children
Ask the children to guess how many bricks there are in the tallest/shortest tower. Count them, pointing and touching each one to develop skills of one-to-one correspondence.

**Follow-up activities**
- Ask the children to find something in your room taller than their tower. Can they find something shorter? Ask them to draw their tower and the objects they have found next to it.
- Gather some dolls of different sizes and hold them upright on the floor. Can the children put them in order from the tallest to the shortest?
- Use photocopiable page 59 to do some non-standard measuring. Ask the children to use bricks to measure the picture of the clown. Count how many it takes.

# COUNTING CATERPILLARS

*Learning objective*
*To develop counting skills, using shapes.*

*Group size*
*Four children.*

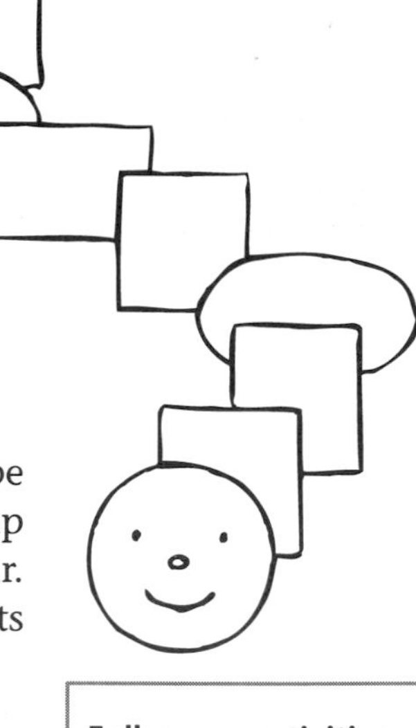

## What you need

A construction toy with geometric shapes, either flat ones such as Polydron or three-dimensional bricks such as Poleidoblocs. Four 20cm circles of paper, felt-tipped pens.

## Setting up

Show the children how to draw smiley faces on the paper circles.

## What to do

Start by sorting your shapes, then count how many of each shape you have. Give each child a smiley face and ask them to line up bricks of one shape, or one colour behind it to make a caterpillar. Now invite them to count them by touching each one and saying its number to reinforce one-to-one correspondence.

## Questions to ask

How many shapes were there in your caterpillar? How can you make it longer? How could you make it shorter? How many do you have now? What shape have you used? What colours have you used? Who made the longest caterpillar? Do you like caterpillars?

## For younger children

Younger children should concentrate on choosing their shape or colour, and counting together should only be introduced if they want to know for themselves how many bricks are in their caterpillar.

## For older children.

Ask older children to stick their caterpillar face on to a sheet of paper and draw round each shape, colouring it the appropriate colour.

**Follow-up activities**

- Read *The Very Hungry Caterpillar* by Eric Carle (Picture Puffin). Count all the objects carefully with the children. Bring in the items from the book and make a display. Use a cornet wafer with cotton-wool for the ice-cream.
- Go on a bug-hunt and find other things to count – the spots on ladybirds or the legs on spiders. The children can make models of these using reclaimed materials. Pay attention to the number of spots they need to have on their model.
- Play a simple 'Beetle' game – give the children a lump of Plasticine each for a spider's body (black is effective). They then have to collect straws for legs by throwing a dice with pictures of one, two or three spider legs on it. They stick the correct number of straws into the Plasticine to make a spider.

# CUBE PATTERNS

***Learning objective***
*To make a pattern with cubes.*

***Group size***
*Eight children.*

## What you need
A construction set which uses cubes of different colours, such as Multilink. Photocopiable page 60. Brightly coloured felt-tipped pens.

## Setting up
Photocopy one sheet for each child, plus some spares for those who want to do another. Make sure you have a flat surface for the children to work on.

## What to do
Demonstrate the activity to the children. As you demonstrate, explain what you are doing: 'I could put two red ones there and two green ones there. Or I could put a red one and a green one and a green one and a red one. What are you going to do?'.

Now invite the children to have a turn. Put the sheets on the table and ask the children if they can place cubes on top of the squares and make a pattern of two colours in each section. When the children have made patterns with the cubes on their sheet, they can then colour the pattern on the paper to match the cubes. Suggest that they experiment with three or more colours.

## Questions to ask
What colours are you using in your pattern? Which colour did you start with? What colour did you end with? How do the cubes fit together? How many cubes did you use for this pattern? What pattern are you going to do next? What would happen if you turned it upside-down?

## For younger children
Encourage younger children to have a go at making a simple pattern with the practical materials without asking them to colour their patterns in on the sheet.

## For older children
Ask older children to draw round their cubes on plain paper and design their own more elaborate patterns. Extend the activity by asking them to work out patterns on 2cm squared paper.

**Follow-up activities**
- Select some of the patterns made by the children. Laminate them and use them as workcards with the cubes for a self-maintaining matching activity.
- Use some of the work-mats produced by Multilink which have animals and objects made from cubes for them to copy.
- Make some workcards which begin a pattern with simple wooden beads. Ask the children if they can continue the pattern to make a bracelet or a necklace.

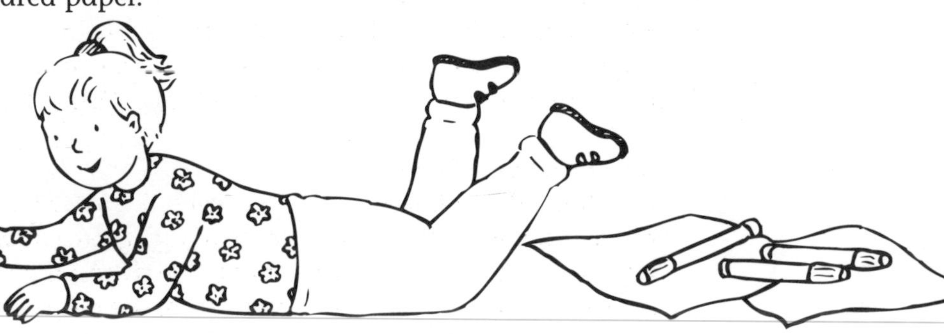

# PERSONAL SOCIAL AND EMOTIONAL DEVELOPMENT

***Young children have to be shown and taught how to work, play, and co-operate with others within the family and elsewhere. These important social skills reach across the curriculum, and in this chapter we will consider ways of developing them through the children's play, focusing on areas such as sharing equipment in 'I need some of those' and taking turns in 'On the bus'.***

## I NEED SOME OF THOSE!

***Learning objective***
*To learn to share equipment with others in the group.*

***Group size***
*Eight children.*

### What you need
Any construction set with wheels.

### Setting up
Divide the set between two containers, put all the wheels in one of the containers. Place each half set on a separate table.

### What to do
Invite the children to try and make a vehicle from the construction set. Divide the children into two groups and explain to them that if they find they haven't got the pieces they need, they should ask the other group politely if they can come and have a look in their box.

Encourage the children to make their vehicle while you are closely monitoring their social interaction. Point out to the children who have all the wheels that they should share with the others and remind the other group that they must not grab all the wheels just for themselves but should share equally with all members of the group. This activity should be repeated with the position of the groups reversed some days later.

### Questions to ask
Who will share their wheels with you? What can you make if you have no wheels for your vehicle? How does it make you feel when you haven't got any wheels? What can you do about it? How can we be sure that we are fair to everybody? Why should we share?

### For younger children
Help younger children to interact with others, showing them how to make a polite request for something and ensuring that they don't just try to take what they want without considering the other children.

### For older children
After the older children have completed the activity, lead into some more discussion about the fairness of one group having more than they need, and the other group having less than they need. You may like to develop this discussion further by drawing parallels between the children in your group and children in developing countries.

**Follow-up activities**
- Make some sandwiches with the children and then encourage them to try to cut them into equal pieces.
- Take your group outside with two bikes. How can they make sure everyone has a turn?
- Play a game of snap with your children. Point out that sharing a game can be fun for everyone.

# A MOUSE HOUSE!

***Learning objective***
*To develop awareness of the needs of other living things.*

***Group size***
*Four children.*

## What you need

A construction set which has long thin strips which could be joined together to make a cage. Examples include Cleversticks and Construct-O-Straws. A real cage with a small animal (such as a hamster, gerbil or mouse) in it. A selection of mouse/hamster soft toys.

## Setting up

Make sure the cage has been recently cleaned out. Choose an animal which does not have a nervous disposition and will not be traumatised by being surrounded by your group. Ensure that the children know they have to take care not to startle the animal, and under no circumstances to hurt it in any way.

## What to do

Invite the children to talk about the cage. Why do we keep tiny pets inside them? Point out the shape of the cage and look at the doors which are needed so that the animals can be fed. Look at the dishes for food and water and discuss the needs of the animal.

Ask your group to make a cage using the construction toy. Work with them, bringing their attention to details about the real cage. Ask them to choose a toy mouse to fit the cage they have made.

After they have completed the activity, discuss with the children how it is only appropriate for a few small domestic pets to be kept in cages. Many zoos now try to recreate natural conditions for the animals that are kept there, giving them more space and freedom to roam around.

## Questions to ask

What would happen if the bars on your cage were too far apart? What would you like to have as a pet at home? Who would look after it? What happens if an animal has no food or no water? What would happen to you?

## For younger children

Encourage younger children to look closely at the animal in its cage and talk to them about the animal's needs. Allow them some free play with the construction toy.

## For older children

Invite older children to use other materials in addition to the construction toy to achieve a more realistic result. Provide them with card, adhesive and other craft materials such as plastic-coated wire to create their cages.

**Follow-up activities**

- Make a large cardboard box into a cage for humans. What do they need inside it? Suggest that the children use construction sets to make facilities for the cage and play with it in the role-play area.
- Can the children build a box from LEGO to carry a sick pet to the vet's?
- Invite a vet to come in and talk to the children about caring for animals.

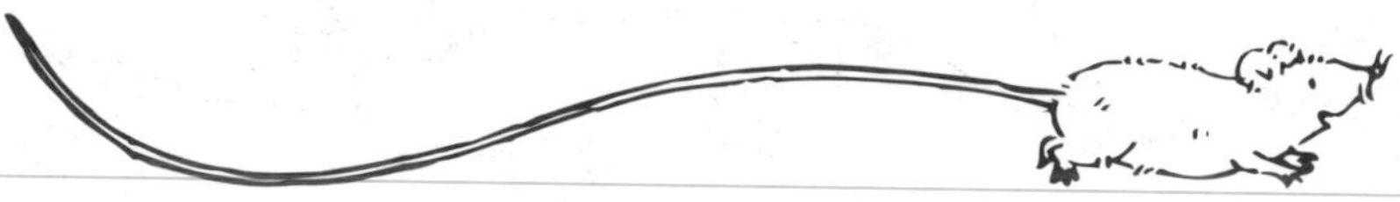

# KIM'S GAME

***Learning objective***
*To develop concentration skills.*

***Group size***
*Four children.*

## What you need

Four very different figures or heads from a construction set such as Poly-M or Luna Park. A tray, a cloth or screen to hide the tray from the children while you remove one of the figures.

## Setting up

Arrange the figures on the tray with plenty of space between them. Placing them close to the four corners will make it easier for the children to remember.

## What to do

Show the children the figures on the tray. Talk about the position of the figures next to each other and point out distinguishing characteristics such as clothing, names, features and so on. Encourage the children to lift the figures and put them down in their places again.

Cover the tray so that the children can't see the figures, and carefully remove one. Show the children the tray with the figure missing and ask if they can tell you which one it was. Replace the figure and repeat the game until everyone has had a turn.

## Questions to ask

Which figure was next to this one when we looked at it before? What did it look like? What colour was it? How do you remember where each figure is? What else can you remember? What else could we use to play this game?

## For younger children

Limit the number of objects to four or five for younger children and space them well apart. Encourage them to point to the space where the object was. What can they remember about it?

## For older children

Increase the difficulty of this game for older children by using a larger amount of objects and making all the objects fairly similar, using just one colour and different shapes, for instance.

**Follow-up activities**
- Play the game using just one sense, such as touch or sound. Choose objects which feel or sound very different.
- Play a card game of 'pairs' or Pelmanism, seeing if the children can remember the position of matching cards. The cards could be made from two copies of a construction toy catalogue.
- Use photocopiable page 61 and ask the children to draw the missing piece of the picture.

# CAN YOU DO THIS?

*Learning objective*
*To solve a simple practical problem – how to join two pieces of construction with a nut and a bolt.*

*Group size*
*Six children.*

## What you need

A construction toy which has nuts and bolts such as Baufix, Brio-Mec or LEGO Toolo.

## Setting up

Make two pieces of a model which can be joined together by a nut with a bolt on it. Do not fasten them together.

## What to do

Sit on the floor with a group of children and play with the construction set. Keep your model to one side. After a while, ask the children if they know how to join the two pieces of your model together. Wait for them to suggest using a nut and a bolt. Pretend that you need their help because you can't seem to do it properly and would like someone to show you how it's done.

## Questions to ask

How can I fix these two pieces together? Where does the bolt go? How do I get the nut to fasten? What can you make with these pieces? What is that piece called? What sort of things do you find difficult? What do you find easy?

## For younger children

Select just the nuts and bolts at first for the younger children and let them practise fastening and unfastening them. Then introduce the rest of the construction set and let them play freely with it.

## For older children

Mount and laminate some pictures of construction from suppliers' catalogues for older children to try and copy. Many construction sets provide workcards for this purpose but catalogue pictures are often more challenging. Draw the children's attention to details such as shape and colour.

**Follow-up activities**

- Set up a problem-solving table with old padlocks, pieces of clockwork, spanners and various screws, bolts, washers and nuts for the children to experiment with. (CARE! Make sure the children are supervised when using these materials.)
- Explore different ways of joining things together such as, sticking, bolting and tying.
- Show the children how to use tools with the construction toys, have a session practising how to use screwdrivers, spanners and so on.

# RAILWAY ENTHUSIASTS

*Learning objective*
*To develop confidence in a group situation.*

*Group size*
*Six children.*

## What you need
Several construction sets, a railway set with an engine for each child, a carpeted area.

## Setting up
Take your group, with sufficient adult helpers on a short journey on a local train. Point out all the different buildings they see alongside the railway track.

## What to do
Talk about your outing with the children once you are back in your base. Let the children choose a construction toy that they think will be suitable for building models of the things that they saw from the train.

Help the children to assemble the railway track. Tell the children that when they have made their models they can show them to the other children explaining what it is and how they made it. As the children work, remind them of the bridges, stations and tunnels they saw on the railway. When their models are finished, encourage each child in turn to stand up and tell the group about what they have made. Accept if a child does not want to do this the first time you offer, but be sure to ask them again when others have had a turn.

## Questions to ask
What did you see when we went on the train journey? What did you like best? What have you made? Where did you see one of those? What is it used for? How did you make it? Who helped you? What can you tell us about it?

## For younger children
Work beside younger children as they make their models and encourage them to tell you about what they are doing, rather than expecting them to explain it to the whole group.

## For older children
Invite older children to draw out a circuit of track and include drawings of the things they saw from the train. As well as describing their model and its purpose, older children could also compare their drawings to the actual result.

**Follow-up activities**
- Make a landscape for the railway track using reclaimed materials such as sponges on sticks for trees, boxes for houses and so on.
- Have regular sessions where the children talk to other members of the group about things they have made or brought from home.
- Paint a railway track on your outdoor play area and use large construction toys such as Edra or Quadro to build bridges and tunnels for the children to go through on bikes or with prams.

# STARSHIP

*Learning objective*
*To use construction toys to develop independence.*

*Group size*
*Four children.*

## What you need

Construction toys stored in individual containers so that children can choose and retrieve them with ease. A very large cardboard box, silver foil, tabards and head-dresses for the crew. A piece of card 25cm long and 10cm deep, a black marker-pen.

## Setting up

Cover the cardboard box with the foil, and put a sign saying 'Starship' on the side.

## What to do

Allow the children some free play with the starship. Encourage them to wear the head-dresses and tabards. Ask them if there are any other things that they need to make. Let them make some suggestions and prompt them with some of your ideas – suggest that they need to have communicators and lasers. Invite them to make these things from the construction toys.

Encourage the children to make their own choice of construction toy, to work independently and finally to put the toy back into storage themselves when they are happy with what they have made.

## Questions to ask

What have you made? What have you used to make it? What can you do with it? Could you use it for anything else? Who are you pretending to be? What does that person say? Where are you going to go? How will you get there?

## For younger children

Younger children will enjoy playing in the box and may also be encouraged to fetch items to help them in their play. They may need to be encouraged and shown how to replace them.

## For older children

Give older children the large box and ask them to decide what they want to make with it. Encourage them to draw plans of how they want it to look. Can they try and decorate it following their plans. Invite them to make items to support their play using the construction toys.

**Follow-up activities**

- Make a futuristic garden using hydroponic beads and water to grow bulbs or beans in a transparent container so that the developing roots can be seen.
- Make a 'space' background by splattering brightly coloured luminous paint on to black paper with a stiff brush such as an old toothbrush. Ask the children to make rockets from the construction sets to fix in front of the background on strings.
- Make robots and aliens with the construction toys.

# ON THE BUS

***Learning objective***
*To learn how to take turns and share fairly.*

***Group size***
*Six children.*

## What you need
A construction toy with large bricks capable of being used to make a 'sit-inside' outline of a bus. A chair for each child and yourself, plus one at the front for the driver. A peaked hat. A bell to ring to get off the bus. The song 'The wheels on the bus'. A self-adhesive label for the front of the hat.

## Setting up
Write 'driver' on the self-adhesive label and stick it on the front of the cap.

## What to do
Suggest to the children that they build a bus using the construction set. Help them to make it large enough for the children to sit within. Choose one of the children to start off as the 'driver' and give each child a chair to use as a seat in the bus. Invite the children to board the bus, paying their fare to the 'driver' and telling the driver where it is they want to go. Once you are all on the bus, sing 'The wheels on the bus' together.

Each child in turn can 'drive' the bus to their destination, then ring the bell for everyone to get off, after which it is another child's turn to be the driver and wear the hat.

## Questions to ask
How did you feel when it was your turn to be the driver? What would happen if you missed the bus? Where did you want to go in the bus? Why? Have you ever been on a real bus? Where did you go? Do you travel on a bus a lot?

## For younger children
Help younger children to build a bus between them, show them how to share the equipment. Teach them the words of the song and encourage them to join in with the bits they remember. They should then play freely.

## For older children
Include the payment of a fare for a specific amount, varying it to suit the abilities of the children. Use plastic or real pennies and encourage the child and the driver to carefully check that it is the right amount.

**Follow-up activities**
- Make small model buses for play figures such as Playmobil or LEGO people. Can the children make a double-decker?
- Use a piece of paper folded into three. On the first piece ask the children to draw where they boarded the bus, on the next, what happened when they were on the bus and lastly where they got off the bus.
- Read the story *The Bunk-bed Bus* by Frank Rodgers (Picture Puffin).

# MAKING CHOICES

***Learning objective***
*To develop independence in selecting resources and making choices.*

***Group size***
*Two children.*

## What you need
Several construction toys with different features. One should have cogs and gears, (such as Luna Park) one should have nuts and bolts, (such as Brio-Mec) one should have rectangular bricks suitable for building a house, (such as LEGO) one should have wheels, (such as Mobilo). Cards showing individual models which can be made using each construction toy.

## Setting up
Limit the cards to a choice of two for each toy. Place the containers for the toys in a semi-circle and kneel with the children in front of them.

## What to do
Show the children the different construction toys, talk about the different models which can be made with each one, and ask each child in turn to look carefully and choose firstly the toy they want to use and secondly the model they would like to make.

Explain that each child should choose to make a different model, even if they both choose the same construction toy. Give them the opportunity to make another model as second choice afterwards. Allow children to take their time to choose and observe them as they copy the model on their card.

## Questions to ask
Which model did you choose to make? Why did you choose that one? What sort of bricks do you have at home? What else can you make with these bricks? What would happen if you lost the picture of the model you are making? What could you do?

## For younger children
Offer younger children a choice of no more than three construction toys. Provide only a single card for each type of construction set, showing a simple model.

## For older children
Older children will be able to make choices between larger amounts of items, giving reasons why they chose the one they did. Some children may be able to write down their reasons or have them scribed by an adult.

**Follow-up activities**
- Encourage the children to choose furniture for the doll's house or the role-play corner.
- Encourage the children to choose their activities for the day and plan their own timetable with an adult.
- Provide a choice of lunch or snack and encourage children to explain their choice and say 'please' and 'thank you'.

# KNOWLEDGE AND UNDERSTANDING OF THE WORLD

***Young children want to know all about their environment, asking questions about how it works, and why things happen the way they do. The activities in this chapter harness this inquisitive attitude and explore aspects of the made and natural world. Find out about floating and sinking in 'Noah's Ark' and experience the properties of magnets in 'Sticking together!'.***

# WEE WILLIE WINKIE

***Learning objective***
*To recognise and explore a feature of the made world.*

***Group size***
*Four children.*

## What you need

A set of stairs in your environment. A dolls' house. The nursery rhyme 'Wee Willie Winkie', such as in *Rub-a-Dub-Dub,* compiled and illustrated by Val Biro (Blackie and Son Ltd.). A construction toy with rectangular bricks which will fit together to form steps, such as Duplo. Copies of photocopiable page 62 for each child to make their own finger puppet.

## Setting up

Encourage the children to colour and cut out their own copy of the finger puppet.

## What to do

Say the nursery rhyme 'Wee Willie Winkie' with the children. Take your group to the available set of steps. Let them show you how they climb up and down stairs (CARE! Make sure they are supervised at all times). Ask the children to try and make a set of stairs for 'Wee Willie Winkie' to walk up and down outside the dolls' house. This could be an individual or a group activity. Now invite the children to make their finger puppets 'walk' up and down the stairs.

## Questions to ask

How did you build your stairs? Do you have stairs in your house? Where are they? What do you use them for? What would happen if you needed stairs in your house and there weren't any? What could you use instead? Why did Wee Willie Winkie run upstairs and downstairs? What time do you go to bed?

## For younger children

Younger children may not have the fine motor control needed to cut out their puppet and may require your help. Help them to build a set of stairs and say the rhyme with them as they make the finger puppet go up and down the stairs.

## For older children

Help older children to make a set of stairs big enough for them to use themselves, using large construction bricks. (CARE! Make sure the construction is safe and you supervise their use of it). Invite them to illustrate and write out the nursery rhyme.

**Follow-up activities**

- Provide a night-gown, night-cap and candle-holder with a twist of paper painted to look like a candle. Together with the children, assemble some low stairs against a wall using large construction bricks and leave them in the role-play area for the children to continue to explore the concept of upstairs and downstairs.
- Ask the children to draw stairs going from the bottom to the top of a piece of paper. Where will they draw 'Wee Willie Winkie' on the stairs – at the top or the bottom?

# NOAH'S ARK

***Learning objective***
*To explore floating and sinking using construction toys.*

***Group size***
*Four children.*

## What you need

A set of plastic or wooden animals. A variety of large pieces of construction which could be used as rafts, such as: Waffle bricks, LEGO baseboards or pieces of Brio-Mec. A water tray, a plastic storage tray. The story of 'Noah's Ark' such as *The Amazing Story of Noah's Ark* by Marcia Williams (Walker Books).

## Setting up

Fill the water tray about half-full. Place the construction pieces in the storage tray.

## What to do

Read the story of 'Noah's Ark' to the children. Show the children the animals and say that these animals haven't got an ark, but explain that they need to have a raft so that they can float on top of the water. Do they think that they could make one using the pieces of construction in the storage tray? Allow the children to find out which pieces will float across the water tray with some animals on board. Suggest that they join more than one piece together and make a raft big enough for all the animals. Will it still float?

## Questions to ask

Have you been on a boat? What sort was it? How did you feel? Where did you go? How does your hand feel in the water? How many animals did you get on to your raft? What can you do to keep that raft floating? Why do you think it sank?

## For younger children

Allow younger children to play with the construction toys in the water tray. Introduce the words 'float' and 'sink' to the children. Add some soap flakes to give a new dimension. (CARE! Some children have allergies to soap products.)

## For older children

Extend the activity by asking older children to make a boat using paper or Plasticine. Encourage them to experiment with different shapes to find out which works best for carrying animals safely across the water tray from one side to the other.

**Follow-up activities**

- Create a 'layered' effect in the water tray. Put in pebbles, wood-shavings and polystyrene packaging.
- Introduce different materials such as sponges, pieces of metal and plastic lids to the water tray so that the children can experience different sorts of floating and sinking.
- Make sets of things which float and things which sink. Put them on a table close to the water tray so that children can continue to use them in their own explorations.

# STICKING TOGETHER!

***Learning objective***
*To experience the properties of magnets.*

***Group size***
*Up to eight children.*

## What you need

A set of magnetic construction bricks such as Manetico. Several large (A2 size) sheets of thin card. Four large non-magnetic bricks. Adhesive tape, thick felt-tipped pens.

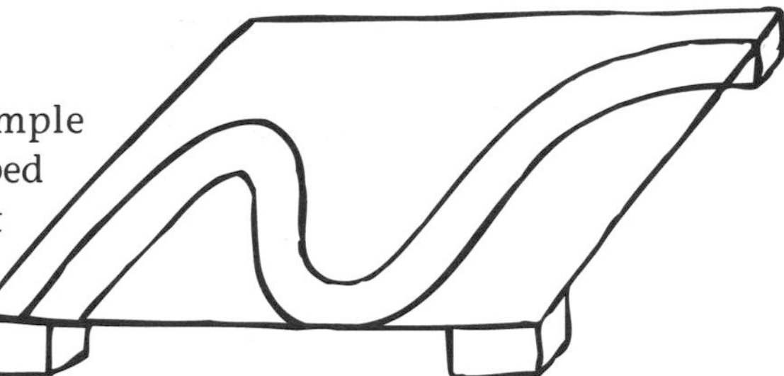

## Setting up

Together with your group, draw a very simple roadway on your sheet of card using the felt-tipped pens. Leave areas of open space. Fasten the sheet of card to the four big bricks (see diagram). Take out the strongest magnetic brick you can find.

## What to do

Ask the children to choose one magnetic brick each and bring it to the sheet. Choose one child to go first and put their brick on to the roadway. Hold the strong magnetic brick underneath and show the children how the brick above the sheet seems to move by itself by using the magnetic force below. Allow the children to each have a turn and encourage the children to design other roadways to steer their bricks along.

## Questions to ask

Where shall we put the road? What can we make this empty space into? What happens at the farm/airport/supermarket/zoo/fair? Why did you choose that brick? What is happening now? Can you tell me where it went? Where do you want to make your brick go?

## For younger children

You may need to play with younger children, showing them how the magnets 'stick' together sometimes, and how nothing will make the two similar poles come together and stick. Let them feel the force of the magnetic attraction which pulls two bricks together. Once the children have had plenty of experience in the play situation, then you could show them how to move a magnet across a piece of paper with another magnet.

## For older children

Invite older children to experiment with this principle of magnetism. Ask them to devise some games – designing base-boards and drawing up rules.

**Follow-up activities**

- Use some magnetic alphabet shapes and boards to help children recognise and spell the letters of their names and other simple words. Many children may have these letters stuck on to their fridges at home, encourage them to play and practise with them.
- Drop paper-clips or other small metal objects into sand and cover them. Let the children use magnets to find them.
- Have a display table with magnetic and non-magnetic items for the children to explore and find in the environment. Provide a tray. The things which stick to the magnet go into the tray, while other things stay on the table.

# ROUNDABOUTS

***Learning objective***
*To experiment with interlocking cogs.*

***Group size***
*Six children.*

## What you need
A construction set which has interlocking cogs, such as Luna Park. Suitably-sized figures. A green mat or cloth. A visit to a local park which has a roundabout would be an excellent introduction to this activity.

## Setting up
Put the construction toy on top of the green mat or cloth.

## What to do
Take the children to the park and let them have a ride on the roundabout. (CARE! Make sure there are sufficient adults to watch the children closely at all times.)

When you get back to your base talk about the children's experiences at the park, on the roundabout. Talk about the way that the roundabout moved. Explain to the children that you are going to pretend that the green cloth is the park. Can the children think of any way they could build a roundabout for the play figures using this construction set? How could they make it move? Play with the children and, if necessary, show them how they can link the cogs so that any cog turned will drive the roundabout around.

## Questions to ask
How do you feel when you go to the park? What would happen if the roundabout went around very fast? What do you like most about going to the playground? What else can you do in the park? Who takes you to the park?

## For younger children
Allow younger children to experiment with the construction toy. Guide them to find out how to fix the pieces together and encourage them to talk about how the cogs mesh together and the resulting movement.

## For older children
Allow older children to design a whole playground, with swings, roundabouts, a see-saw and climbing frames. They could use string and cardboard to mix with the construction set.

**Follow-up activities**
- If you have any old clockwork clocks or other machines which have outlived their usefulness, let the children take them to pieces to see how they work.
- Place the cogs in thickened paint and print with them to make pictures of fantastic machines.
- Make rubbings by placing a piece of paper over a cog shape and using a crayon or a pastel sideways for the best coverage.

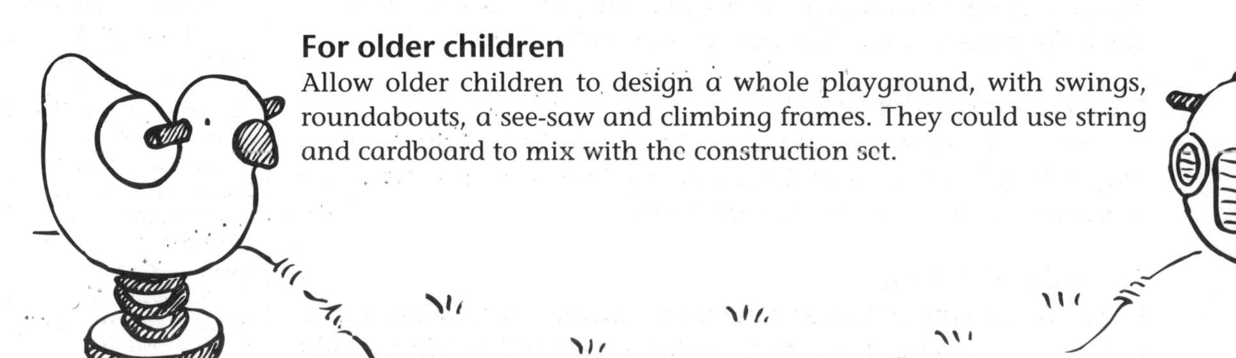

# THREE BILLY-GOATS GRUFF

***Learning objective***
*To build a bridge across a gap.*

***Group size***
*Eight children.*

## What you need
A construction toy which can be used to build a bridge, such as Sonos or Meccano. A 20cm by 50cm strip of blue tissue or Cellophane, a sheet of green card big enough to fit the Cellophane, adhesive. A copy of the story 'Three Billy-Goats Gruff' (Traditional). Three plastic model goats, one large, one medium and one small, a small figure to represent the Troll. Pictures or books showing bridges.

## Setting up
Ask the children to make the river by sticking the Cellophane on to the card, leaving two clear banks on each side.

## What to do
Read the story to the children and talk about the bridge where the Troll lived. Look at the books or pictures of bridges and ask the children if they think they can build a bridge to stretch from one side of the Cellophane river to the other. They will need to make it very strong so that the toy animals can stand on it.

Talk about their bridge while they are building it and suggest that they test it when they have finished it. Will it hold the biggest Billy-Goat Gruff?

## Questions to ask
What are you going to do first? Why are you putting that piece there? How strong will your bridge be? How big will it need to be? What would happen if I tried to go across your bridge? Which of the Billy-Goats Gruff are you going to put on your bridge first? Why?

## For younger children
Tell the children the story, give them the plastic figures and let them play. If they build a bridge, then you could show them some of the bridges in the books and talk about them.

## For older children
Extend the activity with older children by inviting them to investigate how to develop a fair test of their bridge to see what weight it would hold. Encourage them to talk about their findings.

**Follow-up activities**
- Make scenery with construction and reclaimed materials and act out the story as a puppet-show. Use photocopiable page 63 to make stick-puppets.
- Make a simple bridge for the children using safely-anchored planks and stools at a height of 30cm from the ground. Let them use this for role-play. (CARE! Supervise the children at all times.)
- Put the sand and the water trays close to each other but leave a gap. Put the cars in the sand. Provide laths of wood wide enough to act as bridges.

# BUILDING FENCES

*Learning objective*
*To explore and select suitable materials to make a pen for animals.*

*Group size*
*Up to six children working together.*

## What you need

A visit to a farm or a zoo park to see animals kept in separate areas will be an excellent stimulus for language. A construction set with bricks which join together (such as LEGO) or a set which has parts which can be used as fences (such as Mobilo or Galt wooden bricks). A set of suitably-sized zoo/farm animals. Adhesive and a wide assortment of reclaimed materials.

## Setting up

Ensure that you have enough pieces for each member of the group to make their own pen for their chosen animals, and to re-design it afterwards.

## What to do

Start by sorting out the different animals into sets of the same type, then see if the children can make a pen from the bricks to hold their chosen animals. Talk about the different things the animals will need to live happily, and ask the children to re-design their pen, bearing these things in mind and using the art and craft materials as well as the bricks.

## Questions to ask

Where are you going to put that animal? Why is it a good idea to keep the lions away from the deer? What would the monkeys need in their pen? Why? Would the penguins need the same sort of pen as the camels? What food would that animal eat?

## For younger children

Show younger children how to sort the animals into sets and then allow them to play freely with the bricks and animals.

## For older children

Ask older children to design a pen for their chosen animal and then make it, using the plan as a guide.

**Follow-up activities**
- Go on a walk to look at walls and fences in your local environment. What are they for? What are they made of?
- Put the animals and bricks into the sand-tray and let the children experiment with them.
- Include the animals and bricks in free play with Plasticine and modelling tools. Talk about the patterns they make when pressed into the Plasticine.

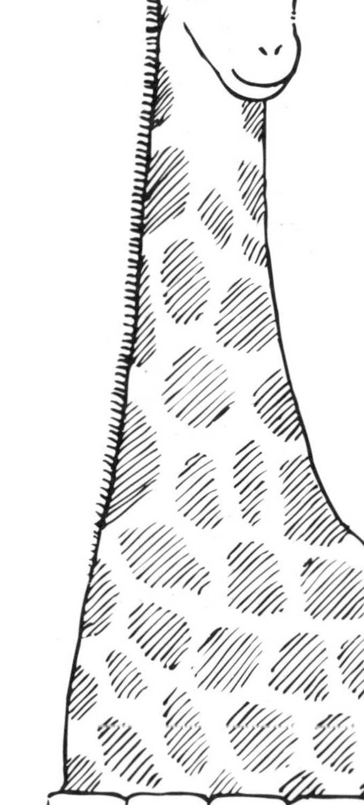

# NATURAL OR MAN-MADE?

*Learning objective*
*To compare natural and man-made items and discuss what makes them different.*

*Group size*
*Eight children.*

## What you need
Eight to ten different coloured/shaped pieces of plastic construction toys. An equal number of natural items such as twigs, acorns, conkers, nuts, leaves, bulbs, pebbles and shells. Two sheets of paper, a felt-tipped marker pen, two trays or containers.

## Setting up
Write 'grown' on one piece of paper and 'made' on the other, put one on each tray. Go for a walk around your base to look at what is growing around you. Talk about the things which grow naturally and the things which are made in factories. Point out examples of each kind and ask the children whether they are natural or man-made.

## What to do
Mix together your plastic bricks and your natural objects and spread them out on a surface in front of your group. Place the two trays on opposite sides, reading the signs to the children. Ask each child to choose an item and place it in the correct tray. If they place an object in the wrong tray, take it out, describe what it is made of and let them try again.

## Questions to ask
Where would you find something like this? What is it made of? What could you use it for? What could you make with this? How do you think it was made? Tell me what it feels like to touch. What is the same about the 'grown' things? What is different about the 'made' things?

## For younger children
For younger children take a walk around the base to collect made and natural items and bring them back to display on a table. Talk about the things that they found. Can the children sort them carefully into groups?

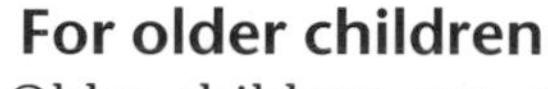

## For older children
Older children can start to consider the qualities of different man-made and natural materials which make them suitable for their purpose. Ask them to choose two items and write about the colour, shape, feel and purpose of each thing.

**Follow-up activities**
- Use an assortment of man-made and natural objects to dip into paint and print, providing two large labelled sheets of paper so that the children can decide where each item belongs.
- Use a 'feelie' box or bag where the children cannot see the objects, but have to decide whether they are made or natural just by how they feel.
- Draw outlines of objects and ask the children to guess whether they are man-made or natural.

# HOW DOES IT WORK?

*Learning objective*
*To explore the construction of manufactured articles.*

*Group size*
*Four children.*

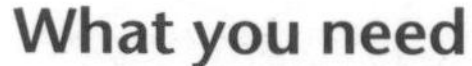

## What you need

Old clocks, bicycles, and other old manufactured items such as telephones, manual grinders and any clockwork items. A selection of simple tools such as screwdrivers – classic and Phillips type, pliers, tweezers. A pair of goggles for each of the group, including yourself (you may be able to borrow these from a local primary or secondary school). A piece of plain material on which parts can be placed and seen easily.

## Setting up

(CARE! Safety must be a priority – the children must be supervised at all times and care must be taken to ensure that they don't use any sharp equipment unaided, or place any small objects in their noses, mouths or ears.) Explain to the children why they have to wear goggles to protect their eyes from danger and that these items may be taken apart without worrying about putting them back together again.

## What to do

Talk to the children about the manufactured items, then show them how to use a screwdriver to open them up and show them what is inside. Talk about what they can see.

Encourage the children to experiment with taking the clocks and other items to pieces, putting all the pieces together on their cloth. Look at the pieces and talk about their shape and colour. It is very unlikely that the children will be able to put the pieces back again, but they may want to try. Allow the children to have further attempts at putting the equipment back together in another session.

## Questions to ask

How do you think we can get this open? What should we use? What can you see inside? Where does that piece fit? Where are you going to put that? Do you think you can mend it? What are you going to do now?

## For younger children

Encourage younger children to practise with a construction set with simple tools such as Brio-Mec or Toolo. Make some construction models in advance for them to take to pieces. Invite them to make a model for their friend to take apart.

## For older children

Invite older children to construct a moving model using cogs and gears, using a construction set such as Georello, Luna Park or Rotello. Help them to make their own cogs from reclaimed materials, such as cardboard circles and split pins.

**Follow-up activities**

- Make a collage picture using all the parts the children have dismantled.
- Stick some of the more attractive parts onto a sheet of thick card and let the children make rubbings of them using soft wax crayons.
- Provide slabs of wood with holes drilled in it. (CARE!) Let the children practice screwing and unscrewing different sizes of screws.

# PHYSICAL DEVELOPMENT

***Young children need to be provided with many experiences that will develop their physical co-ordination both in terms of their fine and gross motor skills. Co-ordination of hand and eye plays a large part in the ability to write, while an awareness of spatial relationships is important for reading. Amongst other things, the children will learn to stride and balance in 'Stepping stones' and will develop fine motor co-ordination in 'Wrap it up!'.***

## STEPPING STONES

***Learning objective***
*To develop striding and balancing skills.*

***Group size***
*Eight children.*

### What you need
A set of brightly-coloured strong plastic or wooden bricks – the shape of a normal house brick such as Edra bricks. Two large plastic trays or similar containers capable of holding six of the bricks.

### Setting up
Invite the children to help you sort out at least two sets of six bricks of a single colour. Explain that they must put the different sets of bricks into containers to keep them separate.

### What to do
Arrange one set of the bricks in a straight line, placing them a child's-step apart. Encourage the children to walk across the line of bricks one at a time, holding your hand if necessary. Show them how walking with their arms out to the side will help them to balance. Once they have done this successfully several times, add bricks of another colour and let the children choose which pathway they want to follow.

### Questions to ask
Which brick do you want to step on next? What colour is it? How many turns have you had now? Whose turn is it next? What would happen if the bricks were further apart?

### For younger children
Let younger children concentrate on walking along the row of bricks, perhaps starting with four to begin with and building up to six.

### For older children
For older children, add more bricks and more colours, mix them up and then ask the child to name the colour he is going to follow from one end to the other. This will involve stepping sideways and larger strides, so will require more skill.

**Follow-up activities**
- Instead of bricks, use hoops and ask the children to jump from hoop to hoop and crawl through them instead of walking over them.
- Put a rope along the ground on your outside play area. Encourage the children to balance along this 'tightrope'.
- Show the children how to balance a book or a bean-bag on their heads when walking. What happens when you bend down?

# OBSTACLE COURSE

***Learning objective***
*To move confidently and in a controlled manner around a circuit.*

***Group size***
*Eight children.*

## What you need
A large construction toy which can be used to create barriers for children to overcome. Examples are Galt extra large wooden bricks, Edra and Balancing Beams. A board/easel to use for planning. A large area where children can move freely.

## Setting up
Children should be barefoot or wear plimsolls when doing this activity. They should also wear suitable, non-restrictive clothing – such as shorts and T-shirts or leotards.

## What to do
Let the children handle the components and ask them for ideas about how they could travel round, under or over them, making a circuit. Talk about the different ways they could deal with obstacles – crawling, jumping, climbing, balancing and so on. Draft the ideas on your board and discuss them, then arrange the bricks according to the final version. Now let the children use the obstacle course for a few circuits. Ask the children if they can think of any improvements.

## Questions to ask
Why do you want to put that there? How would you get over it? How could we make this better? What do you like doing best? What should we change? What else could you do here? What would happen if I made this obstacle higher?

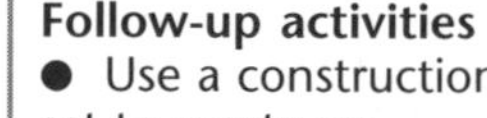

## For younger children
Allow younger children to work with the components and discover what obstacles they can make as they use them. Planning should be verbal rather than written.

## For older children
Encourage older children to make individual plans of a circuit on paper. Ask them to get together in groups of about six and produce a group plan which must incorporate one part of each child's plan.

**Follow-up activities**
- Use a construction set to create an obstacle course for a radio or battery-controlled car.
- Do some movement where the children have to imagine the obstacles in their path, described by you.
- Design an obstacle course for a gardener, a train driver or a pet-shop owner using paper and pictures cut from catalogues or magazines.

# WRAP IT UP!

***Learning objective***
*To develop fine motor co-ordination.*

***Group size***
*Four children.*

## What you need

Plenty of wrapping paper of different textures from thin tissue to thick brown paper. Include some commercial paper of attractive design. At Christmas, festive wrapping paper would be appropriate. Labels made from white card cut to 10cm by 5cm. Sticky tape with a dispenser if possible, but scissors if not. Large simple rectangular plastic bricks such as Babybric. The book *My Presents* by Rod Campbell (Picturemac).

## Setting up

Make sure your sheets of paper are of different sizes.

## What to do

Read the story, which is about strangely-shaped packages containing presents. Talk about wrapping presents – have any of the children wrapped any presents up before? Demonstrate how to wrap up one of the bricks to look like a present, writing who it is to on the label. Put the bricks, paper and tape on a table and include wrapping 'presents' as one of the activities you provide which children can choose to do through the day.

## Questions to ask

What presents would you like to get? Who gives you presents? Do you give presents to anyone? When do you get presents? How would you feel if there were no presents on Christmas morning? Where do you find your presents? When do you get up? What do your parents do?

## For younger children

Provide younger children with plenty of adult help. They will need support to help fold and keep the paper in place and then to cut strips of sticky tape so that the children can concentrate on fastening down the paper.

## For older children

Invite older children to try to wrap the bricks with different fastenings such as string and gummed paper strips. Ask them to decide which was the best way.

**Follow-up activities**

- Include the parcel-wrapping as a part of role-play in the run up to Christmas.
- Encourage the children to find things in their environment which they can wrap as make-believe presents.
- Use photocopiable page 64 and ask the children to identify the objects in each parcel. They can be joined with a pencil line or cut out and stuck next to each other.

# PICK THEM UP!

***Learning objective***
*To develop control and co-ordination.*

***Group size***
*Up to eight children.*

## What you need
A construction-set which includes long thin pieces, such as Construct-o-Straws or Cleversticks.

## Setting up
Remove twelve straws or sticks from your construction set.

## What to do
Sit or kneel with the children and ask one of them to put the pile of sticks on your table or carpet. Explain how you are going to take a stick away from the pile without moving the others. Tell them that the game is won by the person who takes out the most straws without disturbing the pile. Everyone has to look very carefully at the pile to make sure that the sticks haven't been disturbed. The person with the nimblest fingers or most steady hand will win – they can then drop the sticks for the next game.

## Questions to ask
Which stick are you going to get hold of? Why did that happen? How many more sticks do you think you will pick up? What would happen if you closed your eyes and tried to pick up a stick? Is this easy to do? Why? How could you make it easier?

## For younger children
Start with fewer sticks for younger children and practise picking up a stick first, as chubby little fingers sometimes find even this simple act very difficult! Gradually introduce the idea of picking up sticks without moving the others, making sure that the sticks are quite well spaced out.

## For older children
Older children may enjoy this game using more sticks and writing down their own scores.

**Follow-up activities**
- Provide balls of Plasticine together with the sticks or straws, so that the children can develop their dexterity skills making 'birthday cakes' and 'hedgehogs'.
- Make diamonds, stars and geometric shapes with the sticks or straws, wrapping the joints with thread, or sticky tape. Hang them from strings at Christmas for unusual decorations.
- Use sticks and straws to dip into adhesive mixed with paint and make scratchy pictures.

# HAMMERS AND NAILS

***Learning objective***
*To develop hand/eye co-ordination.*

***Group size***
*Two children.*

## What you need
Offcuts of wood 4 cm wide from your local DIY store, some about 20cm long and others about 15cm long. Panel pins/small nails and a box to keep them in. Check that the nails are short enough so they will not stick out in a dangerous way when two pieces are joined together. Small hammers suitable for child use. A toolbench, or a thick board laid on top of a table which can be hammered without damage.

## Setting up
(CARE!) Safety must be considered at all times when doing this activity. Children must be shown how to use their tools with care, and avoid hitting their own fingers with the hammer. Choose a place where the noise will not be disturbing to others – outside in the summer is a good place to work.

## What to do
Let the children practise hammering nails into pieces of wood at first. Show them how to tap gently holding the nail to make it bite into the wood, after which it can be hammered in. Once they can do this easily, show them how to join two pieces of wood together, to make an aeroplane or a boat (see diagram) or any other model they wish to make.

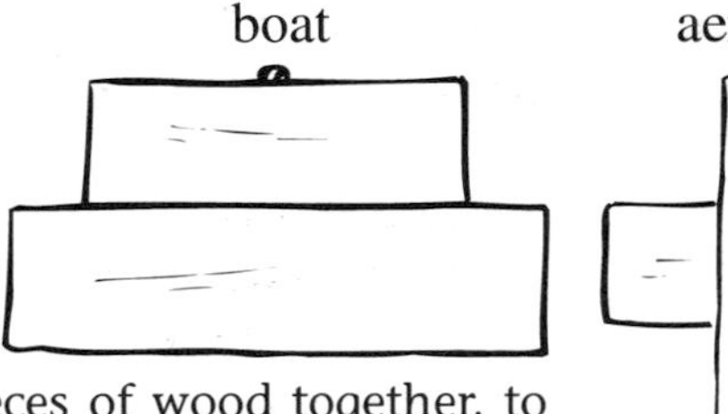


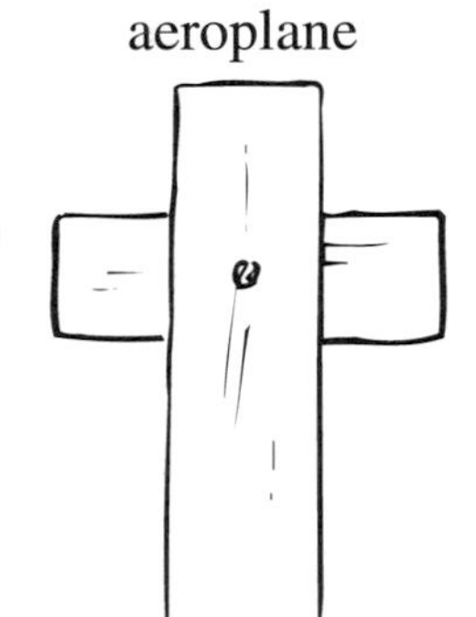


## For younger children
Younger children should not use nails. They should be allowed to hammer blocks of wood, or they could use some of the commercially produced hammering peg sets.

## For older children
Invite older children to design their model before they try to make it. Ask them to think about the equipment and materials they will need.

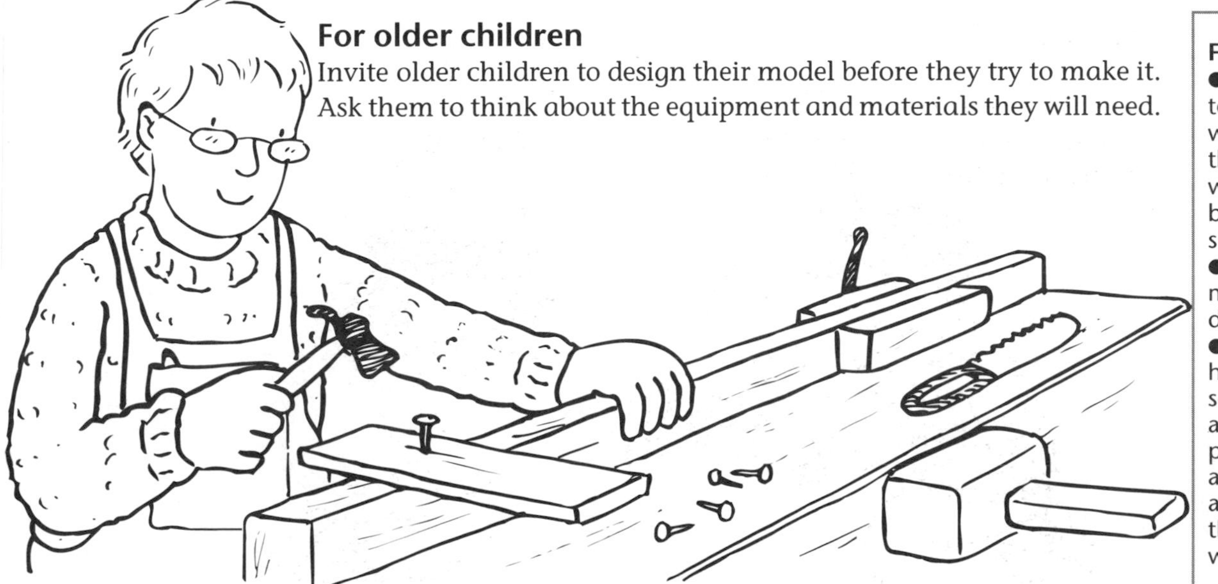

**Follow-up activities**
- Organise a visit to a carpenter's workshop so that the children can see wooden objects being made by skilled workers.
- Collect items made of wood for a display-table.
- Collect various household items some made of wood and some made of plastic or metal, such as spoons, boxes, lids and buttons. Sort them into sets of wood/not wood.

# LET'S GO FOR A RIDE!

***Learning objective***
*To make a vehicle for a child to ride in and push.*

***Group size***
*Four children.*

## What you need

A large construction set such as Edra or Quadro which have wheels and can be used to make carts for children to ride in. Pictures of things which move by muscle power such as rickshaws, bicycles, wheelbarrows, handcarts and wheelchairs.

## Setting up

Allocate a large space for this activity, as children will need to stand back to see what they have made and will need room to manoeuvre the large pieces into position.

## What to do

Show the pictures to your group. Talk about what a vehicle needs in order to carry a person safely. Talk about the sort of distance which could be covered if a person had to push or pull all the way.

Invite the children to build a vehicle for one or more of them to ride in, using the large construction set. Help them to think about what they will need to include and how it will go together. When it is ready, encourage the rest of the group to push or pull it along, taking turns to be the rider.

## Questions to ask

Where are you going? How long will it take you to get there? What else could you carry, as well as a person? What would happen if it came to bits? How did you make that work? Can you tell me what this is for?

## For younger children

Younger children may find it difficult to create a working wheeled vehicle unaided and you will need to give them more direction. They can then experience pushing and pulling in the same way.

## For older children

Encourage older children to design their vehicle, draw diagrams and write instructions to describe how they will make their model. When they have made it, ask them to modify their model to see if they can make it work better. What could they improve?

**Follow-up activities**

- Make a pram for the dolls to ride in, using a different construction set.
- Read *Topsy and Tim Ride Their Bikes* by Jean and Gareth Adamson (Blackie Children's Books).
- Make a bar chart of the different types of vehicle the children have travelled in.

# HAVE A HEART!

***Learning objective***
*To understand the need for exercise as part of a healthy lifestyle.*

***Group size***
*Six children.*

## What you need
A construction set which can be used to create barriers for the children to jump over. A stethoscope would be wonderful, but some empty yoghurt cartons will do.

## Setting up
Make sure you have enough room for the children to run and jump safely. Make sure that the children are dressed suitably and are either barefoot or wearing plimsolls.

## What to do
Talk to the children about their hearts. Tell them that their hearts are about the size of their clenched fist, and that they need exercise to stay healthy. Help the children to build some small barriers. Let the children listen to their hearts and show them how to take their pulses, then ask them to jump over the barriers, backwards and forwards, for about a minute.

Now let them listen to their hearts and take their pulses again. Do they notice anything different? Explain that when they exercise their body they are exercising their hearts and making themselves healthier.

## Questions to ask
What can you hear? What can you feel? What do you think is causing that? What would happen if you didn't exercise? How do you feel after you have done all those jumps? What can you hear when you listen to your/your friend's chest?

## For younger children
Invite younger children to jump over lines on the floor or simply to jump, up and down on the spot to speed up their pulse, as they may not have developed the skill of jumping over an object. They will enjoy listening to their heartbeat in the same way.

## For older children
Older children could try to count the number of beats in a minute, before and after exercise. They could also increase the height of the jumps and see if this affects their pulse.

**Follow-up activities**
- Organise your role-play area into an aerobics studio with music tapes and Lycra fitness clothes.
- Talk about the food we should eat to keep our hearts healthy. Make a collection of packets of food and sort into 'eat lots of' and 'eat just a little of'.

# HELTER SKELTER

***Learning objective***
*To develop the ability to climb and slide freely.*

***Group size***
*Six children.*

## What you need

A large construction set such as Snap Land which has components suitable for making a slide. A mat to land on.

## Setting up

Visit a playground which has a slide and let the children have a go at sliding (CARE! Make sure there is close adult supervision). Back at your base, lay out all the pieces needed to make the slide.

## What to do

Talk to the children about what they have seen and what they did. Ask them if they think they can make a slide for themselves using the pieces of construction. Allow them to try, giving advice and support when necessary. Finally, check the slide for safety, making sure the mat is in place, and let the children climb up and slide down as they wish (CARE! Make sure an adult is present at all times and that the children are using it sensibly). As the children use the slide, describe their actions. When the child is at the top of the slide, say things like: 'Oh you're up high!' and when they slide: 'You're coming down. Whoosh – now you're at the bottom!'.

## Questions to ask

What did you do in the playground? Where does that piece go? What will you do now? What would happen if we didn't have a mat? How would we feel then? How do you feel when you slide down? What do you do when you get to the bottom? What do you like doing best?

## For younger children

Younger children will need more adult support to make the slide. Only intervene when necessary, to encourage the skills of independent building. Hold their hands at first and gently persuade them to let go of the sides of the slide.

## For older children

Encourage older children to be imaginative in their use of the slide – ensuring that they are aware of their safety at all times. They may like to build a higher slide and suggest that they design a fantasy slide with lots of bumps.

**Follow-up activities**

- Help the children to make a slide for the dolls in the role-play area. How do the dolls feel when they are coming quickly down the slide?
- Take photographs of the children on the slide. Write down their descriptions of how it felt to slide down quickly or slowly. Put them together to make a book for the book-corner.
- Put a ramp into the sand or water tray. What can the children put on the ramp to make a wooden brick slide faster? What stops it from sliding?

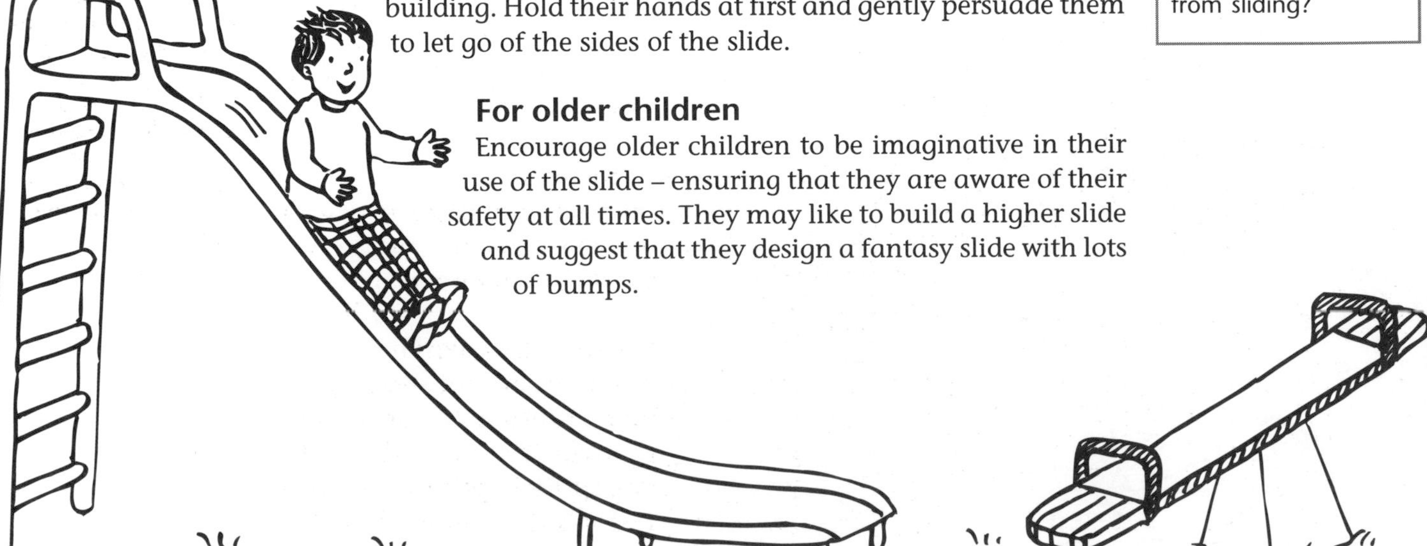

# CREATIVE DEVELOPMENT

***Young children need to be given the opportunity to express themselves through a variety of creative activities. Creative development encompasses a range of areas including music, art, dance, drama as well as creative and imaginative writing and speech. The following suggestions include building a castle, printing patterns, making jewellery and role-playing.***

## PRINT A PICTURE

**Learning objective**
*To print a picture or a pattern using construction toys.*

**Group size**
*Two to four children.*

### What you need
A construction toy with pieces which could be used to print with paint. Sticklebricks give an interesting texture, and construction sets with cogs and gears also work well. Shallow saucers or trays. Paint in a variety of attractive colours – fluorescent paint is particularly successful with this activity. A3 Paper, preferably dark coloured, aprons, PVA adhesive.

### Setting up
Ask the children to choose the pieces they want to print with. Protect your surfaces with a plastic sheet or newspaper. Mix the paint to a consistency which will stick to the bricks. Try it out first and if necessary add a small amount of PVA adhesive. Have one saucer of colour for each brick so that the colours do not get mixed together.

### What to do
Let the children experiment with dipping the bricks in the paint and printing freely with the bricks. Once they have had plenty of experience of this, suggest that it would be interesting if they try to make a picture using their printing. Make a picture and a pattern yourself to demonstrate what could be done. Talk about how you made your picture.

### Questions to ask
Can you make that pattern using two different colours? What are you going to make a picture of? How are you going to do it? What shape are you using? What does that look like? What will you do next?

### For younger children
Allow younger children to experiment with printing with the paint and provide two different shapes of bricks.

### For older children
Extend this printing activity for older children by providing opportunities for them to develop their printing skills – making string-prints, Plasticine prints and using stencils.

**Follow-up activities**
- Put the construction bricks in the damp sand and encourage the children to press them into it to make patterns.
- Provide gummed paper shapes for the children to make pictures and patterns that look like their printed pictures.
- Put sand, glitter or sawdust into the saucers of paint and let the children print over the top of their previous picture.

# NECKLACES

***Learning objective***
*To develop an appreciation of objects from a variety of cultures.*

***Group size***
*Eight children.*

## What you need
Construction pieces with holes, through which a threading lace can be fitted. Examples are K'NEX, Geo-Links and Meccano. Threading laces, wooden threading beads. Pictures, or examples of Native American Indian or African necklaces which have solid shapes of bone, wood, glass and so on. An unbreakable mirror.

## Setting up
Put your construction pieces together in a box or tray together with the wooden beads.

## What to do
Show the children the pictures and talk about the colours and patterns that they can see. Point out the structure of the necklaces, with the larger 'beads' at the centre, and the smaller ones at the two edges. If you have a necklace available, let the children hear the noise it makes as the parts move.

Invite the children to have a turn at making a necklace like the ones they have been shown. Use the wooden beads for the two ends of the necklace to keep the things from falling off. Once the children have made their own necklace encourage them to look at the finished product in the mirror. (CARE! Supervise the children when they are tying things around their necks and ensure that they take them off once they are playing with other things.)

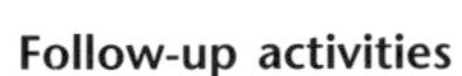

## Questions to ask
What have you used to make your necklace? How did you do that? Where does the boy in this picture live? How do you know? Which colours have you used in your necklace? What was the hardest thing to do? What was easy? Why? What can you see when you look in the mirror?

**Follow-up activities**
- Unusual threading beads can be made by using clay shaped by hand and pierced with a knitting needle (CARE!). Allow the beads to dry and then paint them.
- Raw pasta tubes can be dipped into food colouring (CARE! Some dyes may stain hands and clothes) and then threaded to make necklaces and bracelets.
- Cook some traditional African dishes with the children.

## For younger children.
Younger children may find threading non-standard shapes difficult. If this is the case, just use wooden threading beads or other types of materials with large holes designed to be threaded by the very young.

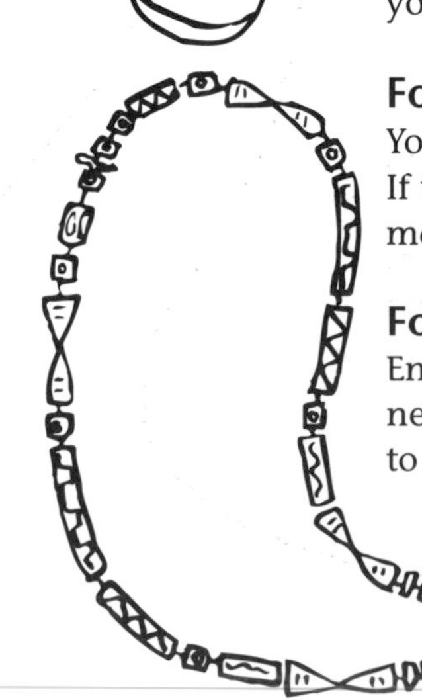

## For older children
Encourage older children to make more intricate patterns for their necklaces, keeping them balanced in descending order from the front to the back.

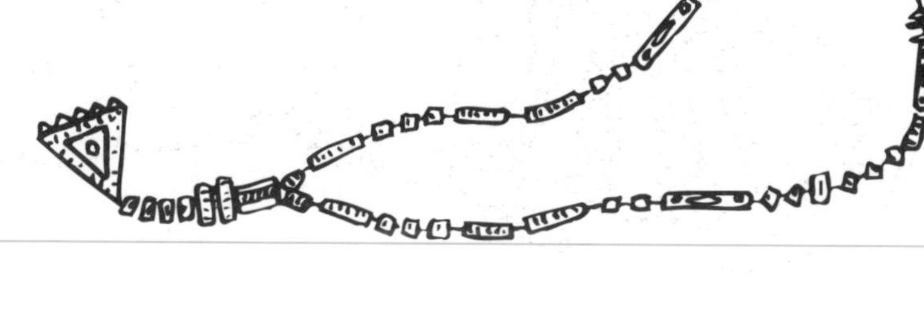

# CASTLES

***Learning objective***
*To build a castle to use for role-play.*

***Group size***
*Up to eight children.*

## What you need
A set of large bricks such as Galt extra large wooden bricks or Ludocyl bricks which have turrets and lend themselves to castle-building. (If you have several sets of bricks, encourage the children to choose the ones they think will build the best castle.) A large picture or poster of a real or fairy-tale castle. Robes and crowns to wear as kings and queens.

## Setting up
If possible, visit a real castle nearby.

## What to do
Look at your picture of a castle together with the children or discuss the trip you made to see a real castle. Point out the special features which make it a castle and not a house. Encourage the children to think that they can build a castle for themselves using the construction bricks. Work with the children, at their direction, asking questions and talking about the activity throughout.

Invite the children to dress in the clothes and behave like kings and queens.

## Questions to ask
What are we going to put here? How are you going to make the castle towers? What could we use to make a moat? Who would have lived in this castle? When would that have been? Do people live in castles now? What would you do if you were a king/queen?

## For younger children
Allow younger children to play with the bricks freely, finding out how to fit them together and take them apart. Help them to follow your directions to build a small castle. They will enjoy using the dressing-up clothes.

## For older children
Ask older children to try to build doors and windows into their castle, or even, with some of the larger construction sets, work out how to make a roof.

**Follow-up activities**
- Decorate some furniture with coloured foil and tinsel to make 'thrones' for the king and queen.
- Read stories about castles, such as *Sleeping Beauty* (Traditional).
- Ask the children if they can think of a story about their castle. Scribe these stories and make a book.
- Ask the children to make a picture of their castle using collage materials.

# PICTURE THIS!

***Learning objective***
*To use construction toys to create pictures.*

***Group size***
*Ten children.*

## What you need

Any construction toy which has shapes with a flat base, such as Duplo or, Poleidoblocks. A3 pieces of paper, felt-tipped pens the colour of your bricks.

## Setting up

Arrange some of the bricks to make a picture of a boat, a car, a person, or a house. Draw around each brick in its appropriate colour to form an outline of the picture you have made. Make enough of these templates, all different, for each child to have one.

## What to do

Put the templates you have made on your table or worktop and show the children how they can fit bricks on top of them to make three-dimensional pictures. Give each child a sheet of paper and ask them to make their own picture on it using the bricks. Once they are satisfied with their picture, they can draw around the bricks with the felt-tipped pens to make their own template, which can be left in the box for other children to play with.

## Questions to ask

What does this look like? What do we call this? Why have you put that colour of brick there? What picture do you want to make? How did you make that picture? What pictures do you have at home? Where shall we put your picture now?

## For younger children

Younger children will enjoy the matching activity but may find that drawing around the bricks is rather difficult. Give them the chance to have a go and develop their skills by free play with the bricks, paper and felt tipped pens.

## For older children

Ask older children to make templates of two or three things to build up a scene, such as a car, a house and a tree. Ask them to describe the way they made their model to a partner, who has to follow their instructions to make a replica. This soon shows the importance of not leaving anything out of the description.

**Follow-up activities**

- Use a sand-tray with damp sand where the children can make impressions of the bricks they have used, and ask other children to find that shape of brick.
- Use pieces of plastic sponge cut into shapes and provide different textures of paint from thin to very thick and let the children print with them to make their own pictures.

# MOOD MUSIC

***Learning objective***
*To respond to music while playing with construction toys.*

***Group size***
*Ten children.*

## What you need

Several sets of small construction toys which have different features, such as Interstar, Klondikers and Lasy. A cassette player and a cassette with music of different moods and tempos, such as *Morning* (Grieg), 'Spring' from *The Four Seasons* (Vivaldi), *The Ride of the Valkyrie* (Wagner), *Claire de Lune* (Debussy) and *Sabre Dance* (Khatchaturian).

## Setting up

Make sure your area is comfortable and has enough space for each child to use the bricks in an expressive way. Provide sufficient bricks for all the children.

## What to do

Ask the children to listen to the music on the tape, and ask them what it makes them think of. As they play with the construction toys, ask them to think about what the music is saying to them. Can they make a shape with the construction which matches what they hear in the music?

Work alongside the children and make your own 'sculpture' with the construction, explain what you are doing to the children. Music such as the *Sabre Dance* may make some children want to push over their construction to make a crash – this is an acceptable response to what is very wild music!

## Questions to ask

What can you hear in this music? How does it make you feel? What are you going to build? Why are you putting that brick there? What are you going to do next? What is different about this music? What music do you listen to at home? What is your favourite music?

## For younger children

Invite younger children to explore the construction material and make a model as they listen to the music. Observe the effect that the music has on their play – they may respond to the music by waving bricks or rocking in a rhythmic way.

## For older children

Extend this activity with older children by asking them to picture a colour when listening to the music. Invite them to collect appropriately coloured collage materials to express the different qualities of the music. For instance, *Sabre Dance* might suggest reds, while *Morning* might suggest greens.

**Follow-up activities**

- Try using music as a prompt for tidying away the construction and other toys. Choose a different piece of music each day and the children soon realise that when the music starts they have to tidy up before they are free to sit and listen.
- Discover all the sounds the children can make with the construction bricks. How many different sounds can be made by tapping two bricks together? Rubbing two bricks together? Hitting various different bricks with a stick?
- Play music while the children paint. Provide pastel coloured paint in one place and bright primary colours in another and let the children choose which they want to use. Encourage the children to move their brushes in time to the music.

# PRESSING PROBLEMS

***Learning objective***
*To explore texture produced by pressing bricks onto a pliable surface.*

***Group size***
*Four children.*

## What you need
Newclay (self-drying clay) or Plasticine. A variety of construction bricks with various embossed patterns such as Sticklebricks, Duplo, LEGO and Wee Waffle Blocks. Rolling pins, a (blunt) knife with rounded ends, or a length of fishing line. Base-boards for rolling the clay/ Plasticine (preferably plastic-coated). A tissue and a tiny drop of cooking oil.

## Setting up
Make a clay/Plasticine tile in advance to show the children, with four different patterns pressed into it. Put a small drop of oil on each base-board to stop the clay/Plasticine sticking to it.

## What to do
With the help of the children, roll the clay or Plasticine into approximately 1cm thickness, and cut into 10cm squares using the knife or by drawing the fishing line through it to cut it like a cheese-cutter. (CARE! Make sure the children are supervised at all times when using this equipment.) Show the children the tile that you have made earlier and demonstrate one of the patterns which can be made. Provide each child with a tile to work on and let them make their own textured tile, pressing their choice of pattern into the surface.

Leave the clay tiles to dry for a few days. Plasticine tiles could be carefully peeled off the board and stuck onto card with PVA adhesive. They can then be mounted on a wall display.

**Follow-up activities**
- Show the children how to squeeze clay and Plasticine through a garlic-press to make fine hair-like strands for them to add to their work in clay or Plasticine.
- Make some biscuit dough so that the children can use cutters to make shapes and then make patterns on them by pressing (washed) bricks onto the top.

## Questions to ask
What are you going to do when you've rolled that flat? What tool will you use? What shape is your tile? What pattern are you making? What are you going to do next? Why? Which pattern do you think is best? Why?

## For younger children
Younger children could experiment with using rolling pins and with pressing patterned bricks into lumps of clay or Plasticine. This is essential experience before they will have the skill or concentration needed to make a tile.

## For older children
As well as pressing indentations into their tiles, older children will be able to add clay/Plasticine to their tile to create more interesting textures. Suggest that they make flower-shapes or bows to add to their tile and show them how to weave a rolled strip of clay around their indented pattern.

# CROWNS

***Learning objective***
*To use construction to develop confidence in role-play.*

***Group size***
*Six children.*

## What you need
A construction toy which can be joined together in flexible loops, such as Polydron. Some pictures/books of kings and queens and their crowns. A real bridal tiara or a child's play 'bride' or 'princess' set would be a good stimulus.

## Setting up
Put the pictures or books together with the construction set.

## What to do
Look at the tiara/pictures/books first of all. Do the children know what this jewellery is called? Do they know why it is worn?

Ask if anyone thinks they could make a crown with the construction set, and encourage each member of the group to have a go. Try on the crowns and see if they fit. Put the construction set into the role-play area and provide royal robes so that the children can pretend to be kings and queens.

## Questions to ask
Who would wear a crown? How does it make you feel when you wear a crown? How did you make your crown? What will you do when you wear it? How could you make this crown big enough to fit me? How could you make it small enough for a baby?

## For younger children
Read younger children a story which features a crown, such as one of the 'King Rollo' stories by David McKee (Andersen). Then play alongside the children during their free play, and make a crown. This will stimulate the rest of the group to attempt to make crowns for themselves.

## For older children
Older children could make further regalia with the construction set, such as a mayoral chain or an orb.

**Follow-up activities**
- Use construction toys to build a palace for the kings and queens to live in.
- Teach the children some nursery rhymes about kings and queens such as – 'The Queen of Hearts'; 'Pussycat, Pussycat where have you been?'; 'Old King Cole' and so on.
- Set up a junk-modelling table with strips of card and lots of glittery remnants so that the children can design and make their own crowns to take home.

# CAN YOU DRAW IT?

***Learning objective***
*To make an observational drawing of a model.*

***Group size***
*Eight children.*

## What you need
A construction set or sets of any kind. Lots of different mark-making tools such as felt-tipped pens, wax crayons, pastels, charcoal and so on. Drawing paper which has been cut into circles, triangles and rectangles.

## Setting up
The children should make a model of any kind using the construction set, but should be told that you want them to draw their model carefully afterwards so that other children can make the same model by looking at their picture.

## What to do
Show the children the different mark-making tools, and let them experiment to discover how each can be used. Then ask the children to look carefully at their model and draw what they see, choosing whatever they think appropriate to draw with. Keep reminding them to look carefully at their model. Show them how to focus on the size and scale of their model, by for example counting bricks and comparing other objects to it. Praise the child's drawing, and laminate it if possible, leaving it in the construction set to act as a workcard for other children to copy.

## Questions to ask
What sort of model have you made? What are you going to choose to draw with? What colours do you need? What shape of paper would you like to use? How many bricks high is your model? How many bricks across is it?

## For younger children
Younger children should be encouraged to play freely with the construction toys, drawing a picture of what they have made if they wish, using their choice of tools and paper.

## For older children
Older children could be shown the various techniques of a particular medium. They could use charcoal, for instance, and use smudging and highlighting with chalk to give a rounded effect in black and white.

**Follow-up activities**
- Do some close observation of natural materials – look at them through a magnifying glass and draw what they see in, for instance, a piece of bark or wood.
- Let the children look at themselves in a plastic mirror and draw or paint what they see. Talk about eye-colour, length of hair, shape of face and so on pointing out similarities and differences in a positive way.
- Look at some well-known artist's drawings, such as those of Leonardo Da Vinci, Durer or Rembrandt. Can the children copy them?

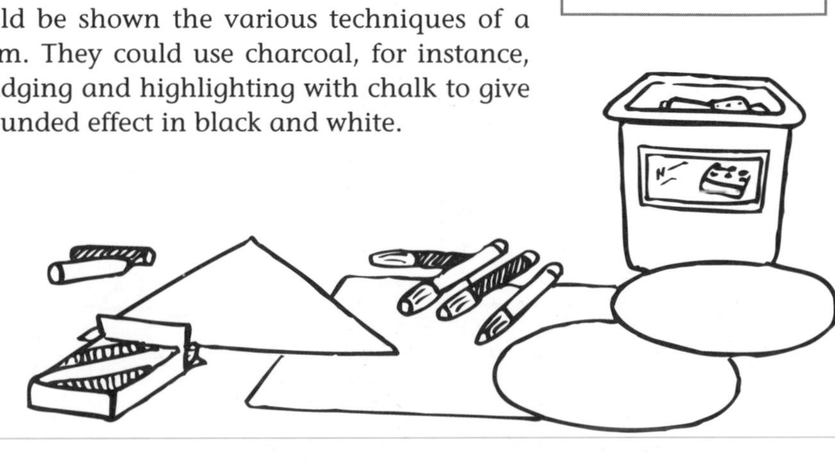

# PHOTOCOPIABLES

Name ______________________________

Name ______________________________

Place some cubes on top of the squares to make a two colour pattern.

Colour in your pattern to match the cubes.

Name ______________________________

Draw the missing piece of the picture.

**Name** ______________________________

Choose the puppet you want to make, colour him in and cut him out.

Name ________________________________

Make these Billy-Goats into three stick puppets.

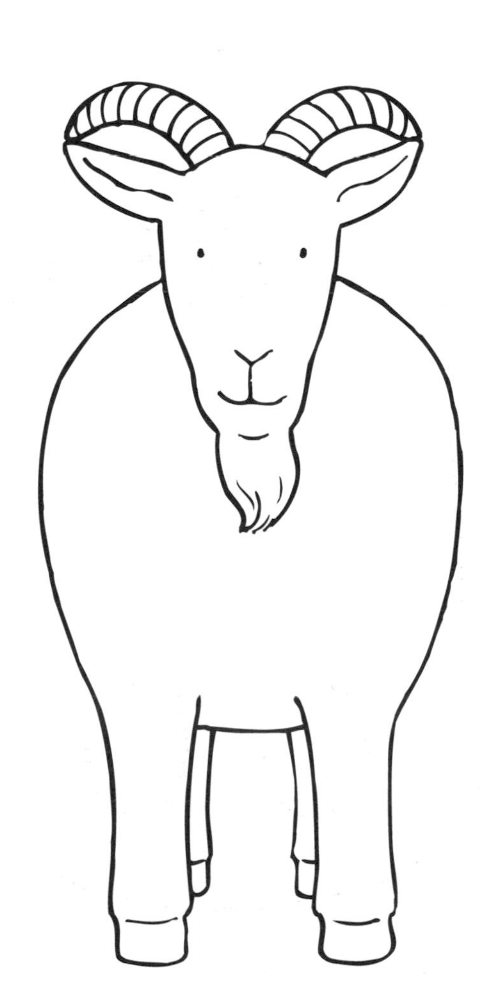

Name ______________________________

Match the object to the parcel.